# DAN TOOMBS

# THE CURRY GUY THAI

**Recreate over 100
classic Thai takeaway and
restaurant dishes at home**

Photography by Kris Kirkham

*Hardie Grant*

QUADRILLE

For Luca

# CONTENTS

# PREFACE

When you think of Thai food, what is the first word that pops into your head? Is it 'spicy'? Thai food is well known for its heat but there is much more to it than that. The recipes are a beautiful melody of sweet, sour and savoury in addition to that spicy kick. The spicy curries I tried when travelling in Thailand were often a lot hotter than those I enjoyed at restaurants in the UK, but they were well balanced and amazingly similar to the Thai food served in the West.

In this book you will find recipes for the most popular Thai restaurant and takeaway dishes. You can make your own Thai meals suit you even better by adjusting how spicy, sweet, sour and salty you make each recipe depending on your personal preferences.

Tasting and adjusting as you cook is what Thai food is all about. You could say that about any cuisine, of course, but to get your Thai dishes perfect, it is really important to taste and adjust the flavours as you go to get the right balance of ingredients. Not only will you be happier with the end dish, but it will familiarize you with the Thai ingredients so that, over time, you will become an expert in making Thai food your way.

I was introduced to Thai food at a very young age as we had a large Thai expat population in California, where I grew up. I loved Thai food so much; it was one of the first cuisines I learned to cook. I was lucky as most of the ingredients required to make the perfect Thai meal were available, even back in the eighties, but that wasn't the case in a lot of US states because there just wasn't the demand for ingredients to make what was, at the time, an unfamiliar cuisine to most Americans. That all began to change in 2002, nearly a decade after I had moved to the UK. There had previously been very few Thai restaurants outside Thailand and the US, but in 2002 the Thai government started the 'Global Thai' programme, which enticed young wannabe Thai chefs to Bangkok to teach them to cook authentic Thai food. The programme not only trained chefs to cook Thai food correctly, it also helped the new chefs financially, through grants to move abroad and set up restaurants. It is because of Global Thai that you can expect to try Thai food the way it should be and not a Western imitation, which you often find at other world cuisine restaurants.

You might ask yourself why the Thai government would want to train chefs so that they migrate. The answer is tourism. The young chefs in the programme not only learned to cook fantastic Thai food, but they also became ambassadors of Thailand and its food, boosting Thai tourism and, over time, making it possible for Thai ingredient producers to export around the world.

Thanks to Global Thai, which is now going stronger than ever, we are now able to purchase Thai ingredients at our local supermarkets. In fact, this programme has succeeded in getting Thai food products far beyond the US and UK markets to places such as Iceland and Nigeria. A recent study showed that over a third of all tourists to Thailand cited the food as their main reason for visiting the country.

So let's get started! As with my previous cookbooks, I would love to hear from you. You can contact me through my social channels: I'm @TheCurryGuy on Twitter, Facebook and Instagram. I have also started a new and lively Facebook group, 'Curry Chit Chaat', where I answer recipe questions and shoot weekly livestream cook-along demos. You can join in the fun at facebook.com/groups/CurryChitChaat. I have also filmed many of the recipes that appear in this book for my YouTube channel.

Happy Cooking!

# GETTING STARTED

To help you find the recipes you want to try, I have labelled them with these badges.

 **Gluten-free:** Thai food is great for people on a gluten-free diet as most recipes are gluten-free or can be easily made so. It is important, however, to look for hidden gluten in products such as soy, fish, oyster and Thai seasoning sauces. Luckily these products are all available in gluten-free varieties. This badge will help you find the recipes that are gluten-free or can be made so by using gluten-free options.

 **Vegetarian:** A lot of the recipes are vegetarian or can easily be made so. This badge helps you find vegetarian recipes quickly.

 **Vegan:** Look for this badge for recipes that are vegan.

 **30 minutes or less:** Look for this symbol if you want to whip up a meal in 30 minutes or less. Please note that this does not account for the time required to make curry pastes or for passive work such as marinating or stewing.

 **Fermenting, marinating or soaking time:** Just follow the preparation instructions and let nature take its course. I have included this badge so that you know you will need to do a little advance preparation.

 **Low and slow:** Longer cooking times are required for these recipes.

# BASIC PRINCIPLES

Making Thai food is all about achieving the right balance of sweet, sour, salty and spicy flavours, so it is crucial that you taste the dish as you cook or prepare it. Using different soy sauces, curry pastes, chillies, etc. can greatly affect the taste. By snacking as you cook, you will get the right balance for your tastes.

Adapting the recipes to your preferences is key. When you go out for a Thai meal, you can usually order popular sauces with your choice of main ingredient. When cooking these recipes, you can do the same. For example, in the classic curries (see pages 67–79) I used popular main ingredients such as chicken and beef, but if you would like to make my green chicken curry with prawns (shrimp) instead, go for it. If chicken Panang curry isn't your thing but tofu Panang is, add firm tofu instead of the chicken.

Different vegetables to those listed in the recipes can also be substituted. If a recipe calls for pea aubergines (eggplants) and holy basil but you can't get these ingredients, use something else like baby sweetcorn and another variety of basil. As Thai food has made its way around the globe, chefs have had to use ingredients that were available. You can – and should – do the same.

# STOCKING UP

Before doing your first shop for ingredients, I recommend choosing a few recipes you want to try and jotting down the ingredients needed. That way you will have what you need on hand without having to keep going back to the shop. Most of the ingredients can be found at supermarkets, but some will need to be sourced online or from an independent Chinese or Thai grocer. I always have the following on hand. (There is information on what they add to the recipes on pages 8–10.)

## WET INGREDIENTS

Light soy sauce
Dark soy sauce
Seasoning sauce
Fermented bean paste
Oyster sauce
Thai fish sauce (this tends to be saltier in
    flavour than other varieties of fish sauce)

## DRY INGREDIENTS

Rice noodles (check the recipe to see which
    type you need)
Rice paper
Chinese egg noodles
Glass noodles (also called mung bean
    noodles or cellophane noodles)
Palm sugar
Rice flour
Tapioca starch/flour
Plain (all-purpose) flour
Dried red bird's eye chillies
Peanuts
Cashews

## CANNED AND BOTTLED INGREDIENTS

Shrimp paste
Thick coconut milk
Condensed milk
Salted turnip (Chinese or Thai brands
    are fine)

## FRESH AND FROZEN INGREDIENTS

Garlic
Galangal
Ginger
Red and green bird's eye chillies
Red spur chillies
Coriander (cilantro)
Mint leaves
Wonton wrappers
Spring roll wrappers
Firm tofu

# SPECIAL EQUIPMENT

You probably have everything you need for
these recipes already. That said, if you are
eager to take your Thai cooking to another
level, you might want to consider investing in
the following.

Large non-stick wok (for electric or gas hobs)
Large carbon steel wok (for gas burners only)
Deep-fat fryer
Sharp chef's knife
Mandoline
Cheese grater
Granite pestle and mortar
Sticky rice steamer

## WHY INVEST IN A WOK?

Although you can get excellent results using
a normal frying pan, a large wok will make
cooking easier when deep-frying, steaming
some ingredients and especially for stir fries.

To get stir-frying right, you need a pan
with a large surface area – and woks tick this
box. Their large surface area and the fact that
they get really hot fast helps ensure that you
can quickly fry up a delicious Thai meal.
If you use a small pan for stir-frying, you
should halve the quantities to avoid steaming
the ingredients instead of frying them.

Non-stick woks are best for those cooking
on electric hobs and for those who just want
to cook Thai food occasionally. I prefer using
a large carbon steel wok but these need to be
used on a gas burner or over fire outdoors.
Carbon steel woks are really cheap and can
be found online and at Asian grocers.

## SEASONING A CARBON STEEL WOK

If you purchase a carbon steel wok, it is
essential to season it before using. This will
create a patina (a hard oil surface) that makes
your wok non-stick. Here's how to do it...

When you buy your wok it will have a little
oil on from the factory to stop it getting rusty.

Your first job is to clean that off. Scrub the wok thoroughly with hot soapy water until all the oil is removed, then rinse with clean hot water. Place the wet wok over a medium–high heat for about 3 minutes, or until the water has evaporated, and allow it to cool slightly.

When the surface is cool enough to handle, pour a few tablespoons of rapeseed (canola) oil into a dish. Dip a paper towel into the oil, then rub this oil into the metal. Really get in there with the oil and wipe the whole surface with a thin layer.

Place the wok over a high heat. There will be a lot of smoke so you might want to turn on your extractor fan (if you have one) and open the kitchen windows. As the wok heats up, it will begin to change colour. Some turn a shiny blue while others just go black. Move the wok around and over the heat to get all the sides hot. Allow it to cool completely, then repeat this step one more time. Over time, the surface of your wok will turn a shiny black and it will become non-stick.

It is important to maintain your wok so that you don't lose that non-stick patina. Be sure to wash the wok with hot water as soon as you are finished cooking with it. Never use soapy water as this will ruin the non-stick patina! Wash your wok with hot water only and then heat it over a high heat until dry.

# SPECIAL INGREDIENTS AND SUBSTITUTES

Depending on where you live and shop, you might find some Thai ingredients difficult to source. I should stress here that all of the ingredients used in this book are available online and from independent Thai and Chinese grocers. If you want to try the recipes without doing a big Asian food shop, you can still enjoy great-tasting Thai food using other, perhaps easier to find, ingredients

found at most supermarkets, but to achieve that authentic Thai flavour, you will need to source the ingredients called for in the recipes. What follows is a list of fresh ingredients with explanations, preparation instructions, storage tips and substitutes.

## AROMATICS AND VEGGIES

**Galangal and ginger:** Many Thai food experts will tell you that there is no substitute for galangal, which, like ginger and turmeric, is a rhizome. Galangal and ginger do look similar but the two have very different flavours. Although ginger is used in some Thai cooking, Thais prefer the sharp, citrusy and piny flavour of galangal to that of mildly spicy and sweeter ginger.

The two rhizomes are also prepared differently. Ginger can be easily grated and finely chopped while galangal is woodier and harder in texture and is normally sliced to season a soup or pounded into a curry paste. Although the two plants are completely different to each other, you can, if you must, substitute ginger for galangal. Your Thai dishes will not taste exactly the same but they will still be delicious. Let's face it though, Thai food has many different culinary influences, including Chinese, Japanese and Indian, which all use a lot of ginger and rarely (if ever) galangal, and those cuisines are alright by me. Galangal and ginger can both be frozen with good results but there will be some discolouration; this is nothing to worry about as they will still taste good.

**Lemongrass:** Fresh lemongrass stalks are a lot easier to find these days. I purchase mine from Asian shops and at supermarkets. The white end of the stalk has the most flavour but the green ends are excellent for flavouring soups and stocks or using as skewers.

When preparing lemongrass, you need to remove the tough outer layer as it is too difficult to use and can be woody and chewy. To release the citrus flavour, lightly bruise the stalks before using. If using in a curry paste, thinly slice the white part of the stalk and pound in a pestle and mortar or blend with other ingredients into a paste, as explained on page 13. The citrusy stalk can also be thinly sliced and served over different dishes such as the deep-fried bream on page 117.

Lemongrass freezes well. I often freeze the parts of the stalk I don't use to flavour soups and stocks. Although there is no substitute for lemongrass, you could add lemon juice to your recipes until you achieve the citrus flavour you are looking for.

**Lime leaves:** The leaves of makrut limes are one of the most delicious ingredients in Thai food. They have a strong fragrance and flavour of lime. Makrut limes are also delicious, and you can grate the skin to use in a similar way to the leaves, but be careful to only grate the green part of the rind as the white part can be bitter.

In the UK, makrut limes are not as easy to come by as the leaves. You can purchase the leaves frozen, or fresh if you're lucky, at Chinese and Thai shops and some supermarkets. They are sometimes labelled 'kaffir lime leaves'. Dried leaves are available but the flavour is not as intense.

The leaves are somewhat tough to chew. Just like you probably wouldn't bite a bay leaf on purpose, biting a lime leaf is also to be avoided. To prepare them, slice the thin stem out of each leaf and then finely julienne them (unless the recipe says differently).

**Red and green bird's eye chillies:** Both of these are used to add a nice heat to dishes. Although spicy, they do mellow a little when cooked. Getting the heat level of the dishes you cook right is essential to getting the dish the way you like it. So if one of my recipes calls for more chillies than you think you will like, reduce the amount. You can always add more. Once a dish is too spicy, however, it isn't easy to cool it down.

**Red spur chillies:** These look a lot like bird's eye chillies but are larger and a lot milder. They are often used to add a bright red colour to a sauce or paste. As they aren't really spicy, they are nice sliced thinly to use as a garnish.

**Shallots:** In Thailand, the shallots are different to the small round brown shallots and the longer banana shallots generally available in the UK. Both of these types will work fine.

**Coriander (cilantro):** Although you will be familiar with this herb, I thought an explanation about using the stalks would be useful. In Thai cooking, it isn't so much the stalks they use, it's the actual roots, which have fantastic flavour. However, coriander roots aren't available in the supermarkets or greengrocers where I live so I use coriander stalks in my recipes instead. If you grow your own coriander, try using the roots in the same amounts as the stalks called for in the recipes. You won't be disappointed and your cooking will be more authentic too.

**Choosing vegetables:** When you go out to a Thai restaurant, you are likely to find a few delicious vegetables beautifully presented in a curry, noodle dish or stir fry. It's part of what makes going out for a Thai meal more interesting. Vegetables such as bamboo shoots, Thai baby aubergines (eggplants), pea aubergines, lotus roots and Chinese broccoli really add to the dishes, both in flavour and presentation. You can source Thai vegetables online and at many Thai grocers. If you can't find them easily, no worries! I am a big believer that fresh is best. Thai chefs and home cooks are great at adjusting their recipes for what is in season and/or available, and I recommend doing the same. Most, but not all, Thai curries and stir fries have at least three different vegetables in them. Find some colourful, fresh vegetables and you will not be disappointed.

## LIQUIDS AND PASTES

Getting a good balance of salty, sweet, sour and spicy flavours is the key to great Thai food. These sauces will help you get the flavour you desire. It is best to look for Thai brands of the following, although brands from other countries will work too.

**Soy sauce:** I'm sure this sauce needs no explanation. Often referred to as light soy sauce, it is used to add saltiness to dishes. If you are gluten-free, please note that most soy sauces contain gluten but there are gluten-free versions available. Coconut amino is also a good substitute.

**Dark soy sauce:** This is not used as much as light soy sauce. It is added not only for its salty flavour but also to add a deeper, darker colour. It is thicker than light soy sauce and less salty. Gluten-free brands are available.

**Seasoning sauce:** This sauce is used sparingly but often in Thai cuisine. It is saltier and sweeter than soy sauce. The two brands I like are Healthy Boy and Golden Mountain. I don't use it a lot in my cooking, but it is often used as a substitute by those who don't like the fishy flavour of fish sauce. Gluten-free brands are available.

**Fish sauce:** This adds a salty flavour and is used a lot in Thai cooking. It's made from fermented anchovies, salt, sugar and water. My favourite Thai brand is Squid. When looking for fish sauce, ensure that it is clear and brown in colour. Thai fish sauce tends to be saltier than other varieties and I have kept this in mind with these recipes. Gluten-free, vegan and vegetarian brands are available.

**Oyster sauce:** Although it contains oysters or oyster extract, it is not at all fishy; instead it is a delicious mixture of salty and sweet. Always look for one that has oysters as the first ingredient. Gluten-free brands are available.

**Fermented yellow soy bean paste:** This adds a savoury flavour to some noodle dishes, marinades and stir fries. It contains gluten but you can substitute Yeo-brand gluten-free hot soy bean paste.

**Vinegar:** Thai cooks don't use all the different vinegars used in Western cuisine. They mostly use white distilled vinegar or sometimes rice vinegar, which add a nice sour flavour.

**Tamarind paste:** You can purchase tamarind paste or concentrate to add a delicious sour flavour. I usually make my own from block tamarind because I find the flavour nicer; I've included my recipe for this on page 17.

**Shrimp paste:** This pungently strong, fishy ingredient doesn't smell very nice when raw, but when used in cooking or pounded into a curry paste, it's delicious. The salty paste is used sparingly as it can quickly overpower a dish, so use as directed in my recipes.

## DRY INGREDIENTS

**Palm sugar:** This is one of the main ways of adding sweet flavour to Thai dishes. It can be purchased at Thai and Chinese grocers and online. Palm sugar is light golden brown in colour. It is sold in either hard rounds (which need to be finely chopped or grated before using) or as a soft sugar paste. It is worth picking some up if you can get it. When I don't have any on hand, I use white caster sugar or honey, and I've not had any complaints yet. Granulated palm sugar is available but it isn't suitable for all dishes.

**Dried Thai red chillies:** These are simply dried red bird's eye chillies that add a nice but subtle spicy hit to curry pastes, sauces and stir fries. They are often soaked in water for about 30 minutes before pounding to a paste. That's what I do, but alternatively you can simply blend them, stems and all, into a fine powder and add to taste.

# BASICS

In this section you will find recipes for some of the ingredients you can make at home that will take your Thai meals to a whole new and fantastic level. From pastes, stocks and broths to homemade rice noodles, ground spices and sauces, you'll find the most important and most used ones here.

Most of these basics can of course be purchased ready-made, and I bet a lot of Thai restaurants do just that. Making your own, however, is what is going to make your Thai creations the best they can be.

# THAI CURRY PASTES

Most Thai curries start with a prepared paste. These pastes get the curry and other dishes that call for them off to a good start, adding salty, sour and spicy flavours that you can then adjust with other ingredients as you cook your meals. Curry pastes play a huge role in how good many of the recipes in this book and, for that matter, any Thai cookbook will be. I usually make my own pastes and have done for many years. Not only that, I make them the traditional way, pounding the aromatic ingredients in a pestle and mortar for up to 60 minutes until ground and bashed into a delicious paste. Doing this ensures optimum flavour – the likes of which you will only experience at the best and most expensive Thai restaurants. That said, you need to make these recipes in a way that is fun for you and convenient for your lifestyle. So please read on and I will explain all your curry paste options.

## KNOW YOUR CURRY PASTES

Each of the following essential curry pastes are quite similar. Adjusting the amounts of certain ingredients or adding extra ingredients is what gives them their own personality and colour.

Please note that the colouring of your curries will vary depending on how much of each ingredient you use when cooking. Green curries, for example, could be a really deep green or a pale light green, depending on how many green chillies and how much coconut milk you use. The most important thing to consider is not the colour of your paste but the flavour, so make sure you adjust the ingredients to your preferences when cooking, tasting as you go along and ensuring you've got the right level of spice.

Do remember that the curry paste will be used with other ingredients to make the curry, and probably served with rice, so the finished dish will be less spicy.

As the pastes are similar, you can substitute one for the other in different recipes. You will of course get a different flavour in the end, but that flavour will be equally delicious.

**Green curry paste:** Contrary to popular belief, green curry paste is the spiciest of them all due to the use of lots of fresh green bird's eye chillies. If you like the flavour of a green curry but don't like a lot of spicy heat, you can reduce the amount of chillies used. Likewise, you can increase the amount of chillies used.

**Red curry paste:** Thought by many to be the spicy one because of its red hue, this paste can actually be quite mild. Again, you can make it spicier if you wish by adding more red bird's eye chillies or more dried red chillies. Thai red curry paste is called for in numerous recipes in this book and is a good one to have on hand. Ideally homemade!

**Massaman curry paste:** This is different to the others due to its Indian and Persian influences. The roasted whole spices used are like those used in many Persian and Indian recipes.

**Panang curry paste:** Panang curries are hugely popular, and if you want to get the true flavour of Panang curry, making the curry paste yourself is essential. Most shop-bought versions no longer include peanuts for allergy reasons but peanuts are what makes it a Panang curry, so get in there and start pounding your Panang curry paste!

**Yellow curry paste:** This is the mildest of the curry pastes. It is really a milder version of Thai red curry paste but with added turmeric, which gives it a nice yellow colour.

## METHODS FOR MAKING YOUR OWN CURRY PASTES

Make your own pastes and you will be amazed at how fantastic your curries taste. I have enjoyed incredible Thai curries at home and I would love for you to be able to do the same. There are a few methods you can choose from, depending on how much time and work you want to put in, and I've outlined each below.

Do keep in mind that every bit of work you put in really pays off. If you choose to pound your own pastes and follow the other instructions in this cookbook, I promise you will be on your way to Thai food heaven. But do I cheat from time to time? You bet!

### POUNDING INGREDIENTS INTO A PASTE

The traditional way of making curry pastes is to pound fresh ingredients with a pestle and mortar. This slowly releases the natural oils and flavours from each ingredient. The flavours are more intense and you will be rewarded for all your hard work when you take your first bite of whatever it is you're making. As you will see from my traditional recipes, however, a good paste can take upwards of 60 minutes to make, so this technique isn't for everyone.

### POUNDING AND BLENDING INGREDIENTS INTO A PASTE

I consider this to be the second-best option and definitely better than most curry pastes you can buy, vacuum-sealed or in a jar. For this method, you begin by following my curry paste recipes as they are written, pounding away at the fresh ingredients for about 5 minutes. This way you get some of the benefits of pounding your pastes. You then continue by blending the ingredients in a food processor or spice grinder until you have a paste. This will save you a lot of time and physical effort.

### BLENDING INGREDIENTS INTO A PASTE

This is pretty self-explanatory. By simply blending fresh ingredients, you will still get a good-quality curry paste that will work perfectly well. You won't get the same intensity of flavours as the previous two methods but it's still worth making a homemade paste this way. You might find that you need to add a little extra liquid when using this method – either a little water or some extra lime juice will work well.

## USING SHOP-BOUGHT PASTES IN THESE RECIPES

If you buy a pot or jar of curry paste, you can still get good results, but you will lose some of the control you have over the flavour of the finished dish. I don't want to discourage you from choosing this option so I will put my hands up now and say I use shop-bought curry pastes from time to time. There are some good ones out there but my personal favourite is Mae Ploy. If using shop-bought pastes is the way forward for you, just as it is at many restaurants and takeaways, then you might want to experiment with one or two brands to see which you prefer.

Commercial pastes are much finer in texture than what you can make at home. They are often quite salty and very spicy, so if you use too much, you could find that they overpower your curry. As there are so many complementary ingredients in my homemade pastes, I find that I can use a whole batch (about 7 generous tablespoons) in one curry, whereas I would only use about 2–3 tablespoons of Mae Ploy paste for the same curry. So if you use a commercial paste that you are not familiar with, add just a couple of tablespoons to your curry and then top it up, if needed, to get the flavour you're looking for.

# THAI GREEN CURRY PASTE
### MAKES APPROX. 250ML (1 CUP)

This is one of the spiciest Thai curry pastes. I find using about 20 green bird's eye chillies is the perfect heat for me, but you can add more or use fewer to adjust the heat level. Make sure you taste and adjust this as you go to get the right balance of flavours.

PREP TIME: 40–60 MINS
COOKING TIME: 5 MINS

1 tsp cumin seeds
1 tsp coriander seeds
1½ tsp white pepper
About 20 green bird's eye chillies, roughly chopped (more or less to taste)
2 lemongrass stalks (white parts only), thinly sliced (about 4 generous tbsp)
8 garlic cloves, smashed
1 thumb-sized piece of galangal, thinly sliced
3 small shallots, roughly chopped
10 Thai sweet basil stalks (about 1 tbsp)
5 coriander (cilantro) stalks (about ½ tbsp)
Zest of ½ lime
5 lime leaves (fresh or frozen)
1 tsp shrimp paste

Heat a frying pan over a medium heat and toast the cumin and coriander seeds until warm to the touch and fragrant but not yet smoking. Transfer to a pestle and mortar to cool a little and then pound into a fine powder. Stir in the white pepper.

Add the green chillies and begin pounding to a paste. Add the lemongrass and do the same. Continue with the remaining ingredients up to but not including the shrimp paste, pounding until you have a smooth, buttery paste. This will take 40–60 minutes. (For quicker, less traditional methods, see page 13. If blending, you might need to add a little water to help it combine.)

Once the paste is smooth, stir in the shrimp paste and pound to incorporate. For best results, use this paste on the day you make it, but it can be kept in an air-tight container in the fridge for about a week or frozen for up to 3 months.

# THAI RED CURRY PASTE
### MAKES APPROX. 250ML (1 CUP)

This is one of the most used curry pastes in Thai cooking. It has a nice kick to it but usually isn't as spicy as green curry paste. Don't forget to taste and adjust this as you go along – if you like your red curries to be really spicy, you could add more dried bird's eye chillies. You can also make the paste a more vibrant red by adding more spur chillies.

PREP TIME: 40–60 MINS
COOKING TIME: 5 MINS

1 generous tbsp cumin seeds
1 generous tbsp coriander seeds
1½ tsp white pepper
12 dried red bird's eye chillies, soaked in water for 30 minutes and then cut into small pieces
12 garlic cloves, roughly chopped
2 medium shallots, finely chopped
1 thumb-sized piece of galangal, thinly sliced
2 red spur chillies, thinly sliced
1 lemongrass stalk, tough outer part removed and thinly sliced
10 thick coriander stalks (about 1 generous tbsp)
Zest of ½ lime
1 tsp shrimp paste

Heat a frying pan over a medium heat and toast the cumin and coriander seeds until fragrant and warm to the touch but not yet smoking. Transfer to a pestle and mortar to cool, then pound to a fine powder. Stir in the white pepper.

Now add the dried red bird's eye chillies and begin pounding to a paste. Add the garlic cloves and do the same. Continue with the remaining ingredients except for the shrimp paste, pounding until you have a smooth paste. This will take 40–60 minutes. (For quicker, less traditional methods, see page 13. If blending, you might need to add a little water to help it combine.)

When you have a good paste, add the shrimp paste and and pound for another 5 minutes or so. This paste can be stored in the fridge for up to 2 weeks; it also freezes well for up to 2 months.

**Clockwise from top right:** Thai red curry paste; massaman curry paste (page 16); yellow curry paste (page 17); Panang curry paste (page 16); and Thai green curry paste

# MASSAMAN CURRY PASTE
MAKES APPROX. 250ML (1 CUP)

Massaman curries have many more spices than other well-known curries. They are believed to have Muslim roots.

PREP TIME: 40–60 MINS
COOKING TIME: 5 MINS

1 tbsp coriander seeds
1½ tbsp cumin seeds
5 whole cloves
1 tbsp black peppercorns
1 whole nutmeg
Seeds from 6 green cardamom pods
5cm (2in) piece of cinnamon stick
12 dried red bird's eye chillies, soaked in water for
    30 minutes and then cut into small pieces
8 garlic cloves, smashed
2–3 small shallots, thinly sliced
1 long lemongrass stalk (white part only), thinly sliced
    (about 3 generous tbsp)
1 thumb-sized piece of galangal, sliced into thin rounds
Zest of ½ lime
3 lime leaves (fresh or frozen)
1 tsp shrimp paste

Heat a pan over a medium–high heat and toast the whole spices until warm to the touch and fragrant but not yet smoking. Transfer to a pestle and mortar to cool and then pound to a fine powder.

Add the soaked dried red bird's eye chillies to the pestle and mortar and pound them into a paste. Then continue by adding the garlic, followed by the remaining ingredients up to and including the lime leaves. You want the paste to be smooth and buttery, which I'm afraid will take between 40 and 60 minutes of hard pounding. If you would prefer to cheat, please see the quicker, less traditional methods on page 13.

Once you have your deliciously fragrant paste, add the shrimp paste and continue pounding to incorporate. Taste and adjust the ingredients as you see fit. The paste will keep in the fridge for about 2 weeks and freezes well for up to 2 months.

# PANANG CURRY PASTE
MAKES APPROX. 250ML (1 CUP)

Panang curries are much like red curries but are slightly milder and usually sweeter, plus they have the delicious addition of roasted peanuts. Of course, you can make your paste as spicy or sweet as you like. Shop-bought Panang curry pastes often don't include peanuts for allergy reasons, but peanuts are a key ingredient, so as long as you aren't intolerant, they must go in!

PREP TIME: 40–60 MINS
COOKING TIME: 5 MINS

1 generous tbsp cumin seeds
1 generous tbsp coriander seeds
1½ tsp white pepper
12 dried red bird's eye chillies, soaked in water for
    30 minutes and then cut into small pieces
12 garlic cloves, roughly chopped
2 medium shallots, finely chopped
1 thumb-sized piece of galangal, thinly sliced
2 fresh red chillies, thinly sliced
1 lemongrass stalk, tough outer part removed and
    thinly sliced
10 thick coriander stalks (about 1 generous tbsp)
Zest of ½ lime
4 lime leaves, stems removed and finely chopped
3–4 tbsp roasted peanuts
1 tsp shrimp paste

Heat a pan over a medium–high heat and toast the whole spices until warm to the touch and fragrant but not yet smoking. Transfer to a pestle and mortar to cool and then pound to a fine powder and add the white pepper.

Add the red bird's eye chillies to the pestle and mortar and start pounding it into a paste. Do the same with the garlic, then each ingredient up to and including the peanuts. You want the ingredients to become a nice buttery paste; this will take about 40–60 minutes. (For a quicker, less traditional method, see page 13.)

Once you have a smooth paste, add the shrimp paste and pound some more to incorporate. The paste will keep in the fridge for about 2 weeks and it will freeze very well for up to 2 months.

# YELLOW CURRY PASTE
MAKES APPROX. 250ML (1 CUP)

Yellow curry paste, like the other pastes, can be used in many different dishes. The yellow colouring comes from the turmeric. I usually use fresh turmeric because it releases more moisture and I prefer the flavour. You could use dried ground turmeric if you like. A word of warning: if using fresh turmeric, it colours everything it comes in contact with!

PREP TIME: 40–60 MINS
COOKING TIME: 5 MINS

$1\frac{1}{2}$ tsp coriander seeds
$1\frac{1}{2}$ tsp cumin seeds
$\frac{1}{2}$ tsp green cardamom seeds (optional)
$1\frac{1}{2}$ tsp white pepper
12 dried red bird's eye chillies, soaked in water for 30 minutes and then cut into small pieces
12 garlic cloves
1 thumb-sized piece of galangal, thinly sliced
1 thumb-sized piece of fresh turmeric, peeled and thinly sliced, or $1$–$1\frac{1}{2}$ tsp ground turmeric
3 lime leaves, stalks removed and finely chopped
3 medium shallots, halved
10 thick coriander stalks (about 1 generous tbsp)
2 tbsp sliced lemongrass ($\frac{1}{2}$ lemongrass stalk)
1 tsp shrimp paste

Heat a pan over a medium–high heat and toast the whole spices until warm to the touch and fragrant but not yet smoking. Transfer to a pestle and mortar and pound to a fine powder.

Add the white pepper and pound, then add the dried red chillies and start pounding into a paste. Continue with the garlic, adding each new ingredient, up to and including the lemongrass, until you have a smooth, buttery curry paste. This will take between 40 and 60 minutes. (For a quicker, less traditional method, see page 13.)

Once you have a fragrant and smooth paste, add the shrimp paste and continue pounding to incorporate. Check for seasoning. The paste will keep in the fridge for about 2 weeks and freezes very well for up to 2 months.

# TAMARIND PASTE AND WATER
MAKES 300ML (GENEROUS 1¼ CUPS)

Tamarind paste is a delicious souring agent. It is readily available at supermarkets and Asian shops, but it is easy to make your own and it tastes much better. Blocks of tamarind come in different sizes but the first time you make this recipe, try making it as written; once you know how it should look, you can use larger or smaller blocks and scale the recipe up or down accordingly.

PREP TIME: 2 HOURS

250g (9oz) block tamarind
500ml (2 cups) boiling water

Break up the tamarind into a large bowl and cover with the boiling water to break down the fibres and release the edible pulp. Soak for as long as the manufacturer advises on the packaging. Some brands may require an hour or two.

When the water cools, break the block up with a wooden spoon and/or your hands. Squeeze the tamarind with your hands until it melts into the water and breaks away from the seeds and fibres.

Pass the pulp through a fine sieve into another bowl, pressing down to get all the pulp into the bowl. Discard the leftover fibres and seeds.

Once you have your smooth paste, stir it. It should be about the same consistency as ketchup and pourable. If you find that your paste is thinner than that, you could simmer it in a large saucepan for a few minutes until it thickens. You need to use a large pan though, as the paste will splatter as it simmers. Cool and then store the finished paste in a glass jar with a tight-fitting lid. It should keep in the fridge for up to 1 month.

## TO MAKE TAMARIND WATER
Some recipes (such as the nam jim jaew on page 144) call for tamarind water. To make this, simply whisk together 1 part tamarind paste with 1 part water.

# THAI CHICKEN STOCK
## MAKES APPROX. 1.5 LITRES (6 CUPS)

When making stocks for Asian dishes, it is important to use Asian ingredients. Chicken stock is used as a base for dishes in so many cuisines. Using a Western-style chicken stock or – even worse – chicken stock cubes to cook Thai recipes just won't do, as the flavours will be wrong. This simple Thai stock will get you the flavour you need for your Thai dishes.

PREP TIME: 5 MINS
COOKING TIME: 2 HOURS

1.5kg (3lb 5oz) meaty chicken bones
10 coriander (cilantro) stalks
1 large onion, roughly chopped
10 garlic cloves, smashed
2.5cm (1in) piece of galangal, thinly sliced and
   lightly smashed
1 whole lemongrass stalk, bruised
1 tsp white peppercorns (or black peppercorns if
   you must)

Add the chicken bones to a large saucepan and cover with 2 litres (8 cups) of water. Bring to a simmer, making sure to skim off any foam that floats to the top. Once all the foam is skimmed add the remaining ingredients. Allow to simmer for about 2 hours.

Strain through a fine sieve. This stock can be used immediately but it also freezes really well. If storing in the fridge or freezer, it is important to cool it down as quickly as possible. To do this, I place the bowl of stock in an ice bath in the sink.

## NOTE
You could add more water and a few pork bones to this stock for a delicious chicken and pork stock, popular in Thai cooking. This can be used whenever chicken stock is called for in a recipe.

# PRAWN STOCK
## MAKES APPROX. 1.25 LITRES (5 CUPS)

This is the perfect base for tom yum goong and po tak soups. You could use homemade Thai chicken stock (see left) in both of those recipes, as it is super-delicious too, but if you are making a Thai soup with seafood, this will make it even better. Prawn (shrimp) stock can be made faster than other stocks too. The only problem is seafood stocks don't freeze well, so this is one you should make the day you need it. Buy your prawns with heads and shells on, either fresh or frozen.

PREP TIME: 5 MINS
COOKING TIME: 20–30 MINS

Heads and shells from about 20 medium-large prawns
   (shrimp), plus more if you have them
1 tbsp rapeseed (canola) oil
10 coriander (cilantro) stalks
1 large onion, roughly chopped
5 garlic cloves, smashed
2.5cm (1in) piece of galangal, thinly sliced and
   lightly smashed
1 whole lemongrass stalk, bruised and cut into about
   5 pieces
1 tsp white or black peppercorns

Throw the heads and shells of the prawns (shrimp) into a saucepan and add the oil. Stir well and fry over a medium heat for a few minutes until the shells turn pink in colour. Some of the orange goop that is released in the heat will begin to stick to the pan as you fry; this adds flavour so let it cook and caramelize for a couple of minutes.

Now add 1.5 litres (6 cups) of water and scrape off all that orange goodness into the stock. Bring the stock to a simmer. As you do this, foam will rise to the top – skim off as much as you can.

Add the remaining ingredients and simmer over a medium heat for about 20 minutes, or up to 30 minutes. Strain through a fine sieve and use as needed.

# CLEAR THAI BEEF BROTH
MAKES 4 LITRES (4 QUARTS)

This broth is for use in the wonton soup on page 65. Usually for Asian cooking the stock doesn't need to be clear, but for a good wonton soup it makes the dish. You can make this with chicken, pork or lamb if you prefer.

PREP TIME: 30 MINS, PLUS SOAKING TIME
COOKING TIME: 4–6 HOURS

2.5kg (5lb 8oz) meaty beef marrow bones
1 thumb-sized piece of galangal, sliced into 3 pieces
1 lemongrass stalk, bruised and cut into three pieces
6 spring onions (scallions), halved
1 carrot, halved
1 tsp black peppercorns

Soak the bones and meat in cold water for an hour to get rid of any blood and impurities. Change the water at least three times during this process. After at least 1 hour of soaking, clean the bones thoroughly then place them in a large, heavy-based saucepan and cover with cold water. Bring to a boil over a medium heat. You want to boil the bones for just 1 minute, so watch closely. Drain and clean the bones once again.

Now place the bones back into the saucepan and cover with 4 litres (4 quarts) of cold water. Repeat the above process by bringing the water to a boil again, then returning the heat to low as soon as it boils. Add the remaining ingredients, making sure you do not move the bones around while cooking or it will cloud your broth. Simmer lightly for 4–6 hours, ensuring that it does not boil. If it's not hot enough to simmer you won't cook the flavour out of the bones properly; if it boils, your broth will turn cloudy. While cooking, be sure to cover the pan with a tight-fitting lid so it doesn't reduce down too much. Check it every now and then, skimming off any excess fat and impurities.

When finished, pour through a strainer lined with a cheesecloth. It will keep in the fridge for a few days and can be frozen for up to 6 months.

# FISH BALLS
MAKES APPROX. 30 FISH BALLS

Fish balls are delicious in a Thai soup. You can find them in the freezer section of Chinese and Thai grocers, but this recipe is quite easy so why not make your own from fresh fish?

PREP TIME: 15 MINS
COOKING TIME: 10 MINS

450g (1lb) cod or other meaty fish
3 tbsp tapioca flour or cornflour (cornstarch)
1 tsp salt
1 tsp baking powder
1/2 tsp finely ground white pepper

Using a food processor, blend the fish until super-smooth. This will take 2–3 minutes depending on your food processor. Add the tapioca flour or cornflour (cornstarch), salt, baking powder and white pepper and blend a bit more to combine. To make the paste even smoother, add a tablespoon of water and blend some more, repeating with another tablespoon of water if needed; you want the paste to look really smooth with no lumps.

Pour the fish mixture into a bowl (it will be quite wet and difficult to work with). Fill a large saucepan about three-quarters full of water and place over a medium heat. When almost simmering, you can start making your fish balls.

Wet your hands then pick up some of the paste in one hand and form a fist around it. Squeeze lightly until a small ball, just smaller than a golf ball, comes out the top. Using a spoon, break it off and place it in the hot water, which should be just simmering. Make sure your water does not get too hot, as a fast simmer will split the balls – they will still taste right but won't look great.

Continue with the remaining fish paste until you have a pan full of balls. You can do this in batches if needed. The fish balls are ready when they float to the surface. Transfer cooked fish balls to a plate while you cook the remaining balls.

Use as required. Unused fish balls can be stored in the fridge for a couple of days and can also be frozen. Defrost completely before using.

# HOMEMADE RICE NOODLES

MAKES 450G (1LB)

**Although dried rice noodles (available at most supermarkets and Asian shops) work fine, fresh rice noodles will take things to a whole new level. If you are lucky enough to have a Chinese or Thai market near you that sells fresh rice noodles, you should give them a try. If you don't, you can easily make your own. You will need a steamer and a flat, square non-stick metal baking tray that will fit comfortably in your steamer. I have three such trays, which speeds up the process.**

PREP TIME: 40 MINS
COOKING TIME: 1 HOUR

180g (1 cup) rice flour
60g (½ cup) tapioca flour or
 cornflour (cornstarch) (both
 are gluten-free)
A dash of salt
Rapeseed (canola) oil, for
 brushing

Put the rice flour, tapioca or cornflour (cornstarch), salt and 375ml (1½ cups) of water into a large bowl and whisk well so that there aren't any lumps.

Bring a large saucepan of water (one that will hold your steamer) to a boil. The idea is to have the batter in the baking tray steam above the boiling water.

Lightly brush your baking tray with oil (use a paper towel to spread it over the surface). I use 20cm (8in) square trays and pour in about 70ml (¼ cup) of the batter. You might need to adjust the amount you pour in depending on the size of your tray. Tilt the tray back and forth so that you have a thin layer of batter all over the surface. If you are having trouble getting the batter to adhere to the surface in one thin layer, don't worry: just move on to the next step.

Place your tray in the steamer. If you have holes in the batter, let it steam for a few seconds and then tilt the batter around in the pan again. This will solve the problem. Now cover the steamer and allow to steam for 3–5 minutes depending on your tray and how thick your noodle sheet is. Then remove the steamer lid and transfer the tray to the counter to cool slightly. If you have a second tray you can repeat this process immediately.

Lightly oil a chopping board to prevent the noodles from sticking. Using a plastic or rubber spatula, carefully lift around the sides of the noodle sheet and transfer it to the board and brush the top liberally with oil.

Repeat until you have used up all the batter, ensuring each sheet is brushed with oil before stacking another on top to prevent them sticking together. Cut them into thin or fat noodles, depending on your preference or the recipe used. Be sure to take time to separate the cut noodles and place them loosely in a bowl to stop them from sticking when cooked.

Use immediately or keep covered in the fridge for up to 1 day. The noodles might harden a little but they will work perfectly once cooked into a sauce or stir-fried.

# MANDARIN PANCAKES
MAKES APPROX. 30 PANCAKES

**As you might know, Thai cooking was greatly influenced by the Chinese, which is why you will often see crispy duck and pancakes on a Thai menu, just like you do at Chinese restaurants. These Mandarin pancakes are so good served with crispy duck (see page 48) – something that also features in many Thai recipes.**

PREP TIME: 20 MINS
COOKING TIME: 15 MINS

240g (2 cups) plain (all-purpose) flour or 'oo' flour, plus extra for dusting and rolling
175ml (¾ cup) boiling water
Sesame oil, for brushing

Put the flour into a bowl and slowly pour the boiling water on top while stirring with a wooden spoon to combine. At first the dough will look quite dry and crumbly, but get your hands in there and start squeezing and forming the dough into a soft ball. Knead it for a few minutes to ensure the dough is smooth throughout. Cover with a damp cloth and set aside to rest for 10 minutes.

Dust your work surface with flour. Divide the dough into two balls and keep one covered while you work with the first. Squeeze the ball and then start rolling it back and forth with your hands on the floured surface to make a long dough rope. You will need to move your hands outwards and inwards as you do this to ensure the rope is the same circumference from end to end. The finished rope should be about 2.5cm (1in) in diameter.

Using a sharp knife, cut off 2.5cm (1in) from one end and use this to measure and cut as many equal-sized pieces from the rope as you can. You should get about fifteen but that's not important. Do the same with the other ball and then keep all the mini balls together under a damp cloth while you make the pancakes.

Take two balls and flatten them slightly into small discs that are about the same size. Brush one of the discs lightly with sesame oil and place the other on top. Roll it out with a rolling pin until the disc is slightly thinner than a tortilla.

Place a frying pan over a medium–high heat. Dust any excess flour from your pancake disc and lay it in the pan. After about 1 minute, small bubbles will form on top and light brown spots will begin to appear on the underside. Flip it over and dry fry again for another 40 seconds or so until cooked through.

Transfer to the work surface and carefully separate the two discs. If you haven't done this before it may not seem possible, but it is. You will get two very thin wraps. Cover and keep warm while you make the remaining pancakes.

For best results, eat immediately. If you must, you could store the pancakes, covered in the fridge for a few hours and then just reheat in the microwave.

# CURRY POWDER
## MAKES ABOUT 145G (1¼ CUPS)

**I always have some of this homemade curry powder to hand. It's slightly different to the curry powder I featured in my Indian cookbooks and it's a good all-rounder. Thai food has many influences, including Indian, so a few of the recipes in this book call for curry powder. If you want to make your own, you'll get great results with this.**

PREP TIME: 8 MINS
COOKING TIME: 2 MINS

3 tbsp coriander seeds
3 tbsp cumin seeds
2 tbsp black peppercorns
1 tbsp fennel seeds
1 tbsp black mustard seeds
6cm (2.5in) piece of cinnamon stick or cassia bark
2 Indian bay leaves (cassia leaves)
1 tsp fenugreek seeds
2 star anise
7 cardamom pods, lightly bruised
4 Kashmiri dried red chillies (optional)
1 tbsp ground turmeric
1 tbsp hot chilli powder (optional)
½ tsp garlic powder
1 tsp dried onion powder

Roast all the whole spices, including the dried red chillies (if using), in a dry frying pan over a medium–high heat until warm to the touch and fragrant but not yet smoking. Move the spices around in the pan so that they roast evenly. Be very careful not to burn the spices or they will turn bitter.

Tip the warm spices onto a plate and leave to cool, then grind to a fine powder in a spice grinder or pestle and mortar. Add the turmeric, chilli powder (if using), garlic powder and onion powder and stir to combine.

Store in an air-tight container in a cool, dark place and use within 2 months for the best flavour.

# ROASTED CHILLI FLAKES
## MAKES 50G (¾ CUP)

**These roasted chilli flakes are much more powerful than those you find at the shop.**

PREP TIME: 2 MINS
COOKING TIME: 2 MINS

2 large handfuls of dried red bird's eye chillies

Over a medium heat, toast the chillies in a dry frying pan until fragrant – about 30–60 seconds. Be sure to move them around in the pan so that they toast evenly. Be careful not to burn them. Tip onto a plate and allow to cool slightly.

Transfer to a spice grinder and grind to a coarse powder. Don't over grind; you want flakes, not powder. Step back when you remove the lid to avoid a coughing fit – these chilli flakes are potent! Store in an air-tight container for up to 1 month.

# ROASTED AND GROUND RICE
## MAKES APPROX. 185G (¾ CUP)

**This adds a delicious nutty flavour to dishes. It is available at Thai shops (often labelled 'khao khua'), but homemade is best.**

COOKING TIME: 5–10 MINS

185g (1 cup) raw glutinous rice

Heat a dry frying pan over a medium heat. When hot, add the rice and roast while stirring regularly for about 5 minutes, or until the rice is golden brown in colour. Allow to cool and then grind to a fine powder in a spice grinder. (You could use a pestle and mortar but that's a lot more work.)

# STARTERS AND APPETIZERS

On the following pages you will find recipes for
some of the most common and loved Thai restaurant and
takeaway starters. These dishes are usually found in the
starters section of menus but many will make delicious
main course meals too. Sometimes I just make one
or two of these recipes and call it dinner.

# HOMEMADE PRAWN CRACKERS
SERVES A CROWD!

This recipe gets amazing results! Consider this an extra-credit recipe for those who are really keen cooks and want a bit of a challenge. These take time and work to make but it's worth it. Most shop-bought pre-cooked prawn (shrimp) crackers have nowhere near the prawn flavour you get in these crackers. If you don't want to go to the trouble of making these, I recommend purchasing dried prawn cracker discs that are available at Thai and Chinese grocers. You will get a lot more for your money and frying the discs yourself produces tastier crackers than anything you can purchase ready-made in a bag. A good non-stick loaf tin, steamer and sharp knife or mandoline will come in handy for this recipe. Please note that if you are using frozen and defrosted prawns, you will need more tapioca starch than if you use fresh prawns.

PREP TIME: 20 MINS, PLUS
COOLING AND DRYING TIME
COOKING TIME: 1 HOUR

300g (10½oz) small raw prawns (shrimp), shelled and deveined
1 tbsp Thai fish sauce (gluten-free brands are available)
1 tsp salt
1 tsp sugar
¼ tsp chilli powder (optional)
¾ tsp finely ground white or black pepper
2 tsp rapeseed (canola) oil, plus extra for deep-frying
300g (2½ cups) tapioca starch

Place the prawns (shrimp) and fish sauce in a food processor or blender and blend to a smooth paste. You might need to add a drop of water if using fresh prawns. Add the salt, sugar, chilli powder (if using), pepper and oil and blend to combine. Pour into a mixing bowl, slowly add the tapioca starch and work into a very soft dough. You may not need all of the flour. The dough should be soft and squishy like play dough.

Divide the dough into two balls, then roll them out into perfect cylinders. Lightly oil a steamer that is large enough to hold them both. Place the cylinders in the steamer and set aside to rest for about 10 minutes while you bring about 1 litre (4 cups) of water to a boil in a pan that will hold your steamer. If you don't have a steamer, you can rig one. The idea is to have the dough steam over the water, covered.

Cover your steamer and steam the dough over a medium heat for about 45 minutes until cooked through and puffed up slightly. Place the cylinders in the coolest part of the fridge for 12–24 hours.

Using a sharp chefs' knife or (even better) a mandoline, slice the brick into 1mm slices, or thinner if possible. In Thailand and other hot locations, these strips would be set in the sun, covered, to dry for 2–3 days. I usually place them in a dehydrator or a very low oven to dry until hard and crisp. Make sure that the slices are very hard and crisp so that they cook perfectly in the oil. They should snap when broken in half.

When ready to cook, heat some rapeseed (canola) oil in a wok for deep frying. When your oil reaches 170°C (340°F) you're ready to cook. If you don't have a thermometer, throw a small piece in. If it sizzles and swells up immediately, your oil is hot enough.

Fry in batches. Each batch should only take 20 seconds as they hit the oil and expand and become crispy and white. Transfer each batch with a slotted spoon to paper towels to soak up any excess oil.

Prawn crackers are best eaten within an hour or so but can be stored in an air-tight container for up to 3 days. Don't leave them out in the air or they will turn soft.

# FRESH SUMMER ROLLS
MAKES 8

Rice paper rolls are originally from Vietnam but these days you are highly likely to see them on Thai restaurant and takeaway menus as well, loaded with all sorts of different fillings. Not only are these really good, they can also be made ahead of time, which is always a bonus. Dip them into Thai sauces like sweet chilli sauce, peanut sauce or in this case – because of the prawns (shrimp) – seafood dipping sauce (see page 144). For that matter, why not double the recipe and make all the different sauces. So many flavours and textures! I love it.

PREP TIME: 20 MINS
COOKING TIME: 15 MINS

8 large (about 225g/8oz) prawns (shrimp), peeled and deveined
1 lemongrass stalk, bruised and cut into 3 pieces
1 thumb-sized piece of galangal, sliced into 5 pieces
2 tbsp soy sauce (gluten-free brands are available)
60g (2oz) rice vermicelli
1 tsp sugar
8 small rice paper rounds (14cm/5½in) in diameter
1 small ripe avocado, peeled, pitted and sliced into 16 strips
¼ cucumber, deseeded, peeled and cut into 16 strips
1 medium carrot, grated
2 tbsp finely chopped Thai sweet basil
2 tbsp finely chopped coriander (cilantro)

Make three shallow slits on each side of the prawns (shrimp). This will prevent them from curling when simmered in the water. Pour 500ml (2 cups) of water into a saucepan and bring to a boil over a medium–high heat with the lemongrass, galangal and soy sauce. When it boils, reduce the heat to medium, add the prawns and cook for about 2 minutes, or until pink and cooked through. Use a slotted spoon to transfer the prawns to a plate to cool.

Using the same water, add the rice vermicelli to the pan and cook for 2–3 minutes, or until al dente. Transfer to the plate with the prawns using the slotted spoon and separate them a little so that they don't stick together. Allow to cool.

Add the sugar to the water and stir it around until dissolved. Then pour the sweetened water into a dish that is large enough to hold a rice paper round. Once the prawns and vermicelli have cooled, put one of the rice paper rounds into the water for about 10 seconds to soften and then place it on a clean work surface.

Slice each prawn in half down the middle. Put the halves in a row in the bottom third of the rice paper, being sure to leave about 2.5cm (1in) to the left and right. Above the prawns, place two strips of avocado in a row. Do the same with the cucumber. Top these ingredients with some grated carrot, vermicelli noodles, basil and coriander (cilantro). Fold the left and right ends of the rice paper over the filling to close the ends and then roll tightly into a colourful summer roll. Try to do this as tightly as you can so that there are no air pockets. Repeat with the rest of the rice paper and fillings. Serve immediately or place in the fridge, covered, until ready to serve.

TIP

You can try making your own wrappers by following the rice noodle recipe on page 20 using a round metal non-stick tray about 14cm (5½in) in diameter. Remove the rice noodle sheets and, rather than slicing them into noodles, use the freshly made rice paper to wrap these fresh summer rolls.

# PORK AND VEGETABLE SPRING ROLLS
MAKES 30

Made popular by Chinese restaurants and takeaways, these are another menu item that have been adapted to have a subtle Thai flavour. You need to plan ahead as the filling must be cold (or room temperature) before rolling your spring rolls. To make these vegetarian, simply leave out the meat.

PREP TIME: 30 MINS, PLUS MARINATING TIME
COOKING TIME: 20 MINS

450g (1lb) pork shoulder, cut into thin slices against the grain
6 tbsp rapeseed (canola) oil, plus 750ml (3 cups) for deep-frying
200g (7 oz) Chinese broccoli or young broccoli, finely chopped
200g (7 oz) fresh bean sprouts
200g (7 oz) carrots, grated
3 tbsp coriander (cilantro) stalks, finely chopped
4 spring onions (scallions), finely chopped
½ tsp palm sugar, grated (or use white sugar)
1 tbsp Chinese rice wine or dry sherry
1 tbsp dark soy sauce
1 tsp Thai fish sauce
½ tsp white pepper
1 tbsp cornflour (cornstarch), whisked with 2 tbsp water to make a paste
30 x 10cm (4in) spring roll wrappers
1 egg, beaten
Sweet chilli sauce (see page 142 or shop-bought)

FOR THE MARINADE
2 tbsp light soy sauce
1 tbsp Chinese rice wine or dry sherry
1 tsp sesame oil
1 tbsp Thai fish sauce
½ tsp palm sugar, finely grated
¼ tsp white pepper
1 tbsp cornflour (cornstarch)

In a large bowl, whisk the marinade ingredients together until smooth with no sugar lumps. Add the slivered pork and mix well with your hand so it is evenly coated. Marinate for at least 1 hour or overnight (the longer the better). Bring the meat to room temperature before cooking.

When ready to cook, heat a wok or frying pan over a medium–high heat until a bead of water evaporates on contact. Add 3 tablespoons of oil and swirl it around to coat the surface. Add the broccoli, bean sprouts and carrots and fry, stirring continuously, for 45 seconds, then tip out onto a plate (they should be undercooked at this stage). Spread them out, stir in the coriander (cilantro) stalks and spring onions (scallions) and set aside to cool.

Clean your wok or pan with paper towel and turn the heat up to high. When a drop of water evaporates immediately on contact, add the remaining oil and swirl it around to coat the surface. Add the pork and stir quickly and continuously until the meat is about 80% cooked through – this should take about 5 minutes. Add the par-cooked vegetables and toss well to combine. Turn the heat down to medium and stir in the sugar, rice wine or sherry, dark soy sauce, fish sauce and white pepper, followed by the cornflour (cornstarch) mixture. Cook for a further 20 seconds until the mixture is slightly thick and glossy, then pour onto a plate to cool before wrapping your spring rolls.

Try the mixture and adjust the flavour. Add more soy or fish sauce for a saltier flavour, more sugar for sweetness or even finely chopped chillies or red chilli flakes (not listed in the ingredients) for more spice.

Take one spring roll wrapper and place it in front of you with one of the corners facing you. Spoon 3 tablespoons of the filling into the bottom third of the wrapper, leaving space on each side. Bring the wrapper corner nearest to you up over the filling. Then fold the left and right sides tightly over the filling. Continue rolling away from you as tightly and evenly as you can and seal with some of the beaten egg. Repeat with the remaining filling and wrappers.

Heat the oil for deep-frying in a large saucepan or wok to 180°C (350°F). When ready, add the spring rolls in batches to maintain the heat of the oil – you want them to come out crispy, not soggy. Fry until crisp and lightly browned – around 3–5 minutes. Serve hot or at room temperature with sweet chilli dip.

**Clockwise from top left:** Pork and vegetable spring rolls; money bags (page 28); homemade prawn crackers (page 24); and fresh summer rolls (page 25)

# MONEY BAGS
MAKES 30

Almost every Thai restaurant and takeaway has their own version of money bags. These are really just wontons but fried. Money bags are fun to serve and make a delicious starter or appetizer. For this recipe, I kept the filling ingredients the same as in my kanom jeeb (see page 33) because it's a popular filling. You could of course adjust this to your liking, using more prawns (shrimp) and no pork, all pork, turkey, beef... whatever sounds good to you. You could also make a delicious vegan filling: have a play with the filling for the spring rolls on page 26, omitting the meat and egg. Other vegetables such as cabbage or finely diced radish could also be added.

PREP TIME: 20 MINS
COOKING TIME: 15 MINS

225g (8oz) fresh prawns
    (shrimp), peeled and deveined
4 garlic cloves, minced to a paste
A pinch of ground white pepper
1 tbsp Thai fish sauce
1 tbsp soy sauce
1 tsp sesame oil
1 tsp grated palm sugar (or
    use honey)
150g (5½oz) minced (ground)
    pork
½ tbsp cornflour (cornstarch) or
    tapioca flour
7 spring onions (scallions), 2 of
    which finely chopped
1 carrot, peeled and finely diced
30 square wonton wrappers
Rapeseed (canola) oil, for
    deep-frying
Sweet chilli sauce (see page 142
    or shop-bought), to serve

Put the prawns (shrimp) in a blender or food processor and blend to a paste that is mostly smooth but still has a few small chunks of prawn in it. Pour this prawn mixture into a bowl and stir in the garlic paste, white pepper, fish sauce, soy sauce, sesame oil and palm sugar. Add the pork and work this all together to combine.

At this point the mixture will be quite wet. Add the cornflour (cornstarch) or tapioca flour and continue mixing until the mixture becomes dryer to the touch. Add the two chopped spring onions (scallions) and diced carrot and stir well.

To make the money bags, soak the remaining five spring onions in hot water for 5 minutes and then transfer to a bowl of cold water. Remove and pat dry. Now take a wonton sheet and place it on the work surface in front of you. Put a spoonful of the filling in the centre and bring the sides up around the filling, squeezing the wrapper together at the top so that it looks like a money bag. Cut a thin piece of spring onion that is long enough to tie around the top of the bag and tie it into a nice bow. Repeat with the remaining wonton wrappers and filling.

Once you have your money bags ready, heat about 10cm (4in) of rapeseed (canola) oil in a large saucepan over a medium–high heat. When the oil hits 180°C (350°F) you're ready to cook. Fry about ten money bags at a time for about 5 minutes, or until lightly browned and crispy. Be careful not to overcrowd your pan or they will become soggy instead of crispy. Transfer with a slotted spoon to a paper towel to soak up the excess oil and repeat with the remaining money bags. Serve hot with sweet chilli sauce.

# CURRY PUFFS
MAKES 30

There was no way I could leave this recipe out of the book! Curry puffs are very similar to Indian samosas but these of course have a Thai touch. I've used minced (ground) turkey as a filling but you could use another minced meat if you prefer or just fill the puffs with potato and a few other veggies to make a vegetarian version. In Thailand and at high-end Thai restaurants in the UK, curry puffs are made with an impressive homemade wrap, which looks fantastic but is also quite difficult to do. Using samosa wrappers is much more common and a lot less fuss.

PREP TIME: 30 MINS
COOKING TIME: 30 MINS

225g (8oz) potato, peeled and
  cut into 1cm (½in) dice
2 tbsp rapeseed (canola) oil, plus
  extra for deep-frying
2 tbsp coriander stalks, finely
  chopped
2 garlic cloves, roughly chopped
1 medium onion, finely chopped
¼ tsp salt
2 tsp curry powder (see page 22
  or shop-bought)
225g (8oz) minced (ground)
  turkey
1 tbsp light soy sauce
2 tsp Thai fish sauce
1 tsp finely grated palm sugar
30 samosa wrappers
2 tbsp flour
Sweet chilli sauce (see page 142
  or shop-bought), to serve

Steam the diced potato for about 10 minutes, or until almost cooked through but not quite. Set aside.

Heat the oil in a large pan or wok over a medium–high heat. When visibly hot, add the coriander stalks and garlic and fry for about a minute, being careful not to burn the garlic. Stir in the onion and salt and fry for about 3 minutes until the onion is beginning to turn soft, then add the curry powder and give it all a good stir to combine. Stir in the minced (ground) turkey and fry for about 5 minutes until cooked through, then stir in the soy sauce, fish sauce and palm sugar and continue to cook for another minute or so until the sugar has dissolved. Stir in the steamed potato and then taste and adjust the seasoning. Allow to cool.

To make the curry puffs, take a samosa wrapper and place it on a clean work surface with one of the short ends closest to you. Mix the flour with 2 tablespoons of water to make a thick paste, ready for sealing the curry puffs. Take the top left corner of the samosa sheet and bring it about halfway down to meet the right-hand side, creating a kite-like shape at the top. Now fold the top right corner down to meet the left-hand side, creating a triangular pocket with a small flap. Fill the pocket with a generous tablespoon of the filling and fold the small triangular flap and pastry over to close. Now rub the flour paste all over the surface of the remaining pastry, and fold it into a neat triangle to seal. If there are any holes in the corners, use the paste to seal them too. Repeat with the rest of the samosa wrappers and filling.

Heat about 10cm (4in) of rapeseed (canola) oil in a large saucepan or wok to 170°C (340°F) – or until a piece of samosa wrapper sizzles immediately when dropped in the oil. You don't want to overcrowd the pan so you might need to work in batches. Fry for about 2 minutes, turning the curry puffs a few times as you do, until they are crisp and light brown. Keep warm while you fry the remaining batches. Serve hot or at room temperature with sweet chilli sauce.

# DEEP-FRIED TOFU PUFFS
SERVES 4

This isn't just a delicious and simple starter. Fried tofu is a popular vegan product that can be used as a meat substitute in many of the curries and stir fries in this book. The best tofu for Thai dishes is firm or extra-firm tofu – the soft stuff breaks apart too easily. Fried tofu is porous with a spongy texture, perfect for dipping into sweet chilli sauce.

PREP TIME: 10 MINS
COOKING TIME: 15 MINS

1 x 350g (12oz) pack of firm tofu
Rapeseed (canola) oil, for deep-frying
Sweet chilli or sriracha sauce (see page 142 or 145, or shop-bought), to serve

Take your brick of tofu and slice it horizontally through the centre. Then place it on a cutting board and slice it into 12 tofu sticks. Dry the tofu sticks with a paper towel. This will help prevent splattering when the tofu hits the oil.

Heat 10cm (4in) of oil in a large pan or wok over a medium–high heat. When the oil begins to shimmer, place one of the tofu sticks into the hot oil. The tofu should sizzle on contact with the oil. If it doesn't, let the oil heat up more before adding the remaining tofu. Fry the tofu sticks for about 15 minutes, or until crispy and golden brown. Transfer to a paper towel to soak up the excess oil and then slice the tofu sticks into bite-size pieces. You should be able to see both the crispy brown exterior and the quite porous white centre.

Serve immediately with the dipping sauce of your choice.

# PORK LARB EGG BASKETS
MAKES ABOUT 8 EGG BASKETS

I have made egg baskets many ways but this is my go-to recipe. They are not only easy but always look great. Although larb is the most common filling, do try other fillings – perhaps minced chicken or turkey, or a nice dollop of stir-fried vegetables (see page 87). It is worth making a double batch the first time you try this to practise the technique. A small non-stick pan is essential; I use an 18-cm (7-in) pan.

PREP TIME: 5 MINS, PLUS MAKING THE LARB
COOKING TIME: 20 MINS

3 large eggs
Rapeseed (canola) oil, for brushing
¼ batch of pork larb (see page 103), at room temperature or hot, if you prefer
Sriracha sauce (see page 145 or shop-bought), to serve

Whisk the eggs until creamy and smooth – a good minute should suffice. Heat your pan over a medium–high heat and brush with a little oil. For a neat presentation, as pictured, pipe the egg out using a sandwich bag with a small hole cut in one corner into a basket design. For a more wild presentation, dip your fingers in the whisked egg and then drizzle across the pan, as lightly as possible, while shaking your hand back and forth. Dip your fingers back in the egg and do the same but this time moving your fingers side to side to make a criss-cross pattern. Continue doing this until you have something that looks like a woven basket. As the egg cooks, it will start to come away from the pan, after about 2 minutes. Use a spatula to carefully remove the basket from the pan and transfer to a plate. Repeat with the rest of the egg.

To make the finished baskets, place a generous tablespoon of larb in the centre of one of the baskets and wrap the basket around the meat. Turn it over so that the seam is at the bottom and press down lightly. Serve with a little sriracha sauce, either hot or at room temperature.

# KANOM JEEB (THAI PORK AND PRAWN STEAMED DUMPLINGS)
## MAKES 30

Steamed kanom jeeb are a must-order starter when I go out for a good Thai meal. They're so good! Although they look quite difficult to make, they really aren't. This is of course a difficult recipe to taste as you cook, so if this is the first time you've tried this recipe, I recommend frying or (better yet) steaming a little of the filling in a wonton wrapper to ensure you are happy with the flavour before making all the kanom jeeb.

PREP TIME: 20 MINS
COOKING TIME: 10 MINS

225g (8oz) fresh prawns (shrimp), peeled and deveined
4 garlic cloves, minced
A pinch of ground white pepper
1 tbsp Thai fish sauce
1 tbsp soy sauce
1 tsp sesame oil
1 tsp grated palm sugar or honey
150g (5½oz) minced (ground) pork
½ tbsp cornflour (cornstarch) or tapioca flour
2 spring onions (scallions), finely chopped
30 wonton wrappers (round are best but you can use square wrappers with the corners chopped off)
1 carrot, peeled and finely diced, to garnish

## FOR THE DIPPING SAUCE
3 tbsp soy sauce
1½ tsp dark soy sauce
1 tbsp sriracha sauce (see page 145 or shop-bought)
2 tbsp vinegar
1 tsp sugar (optional)

Put the prawns (shrimp) into a food processor and blend – you want a coarse paste but you should still see a few small pieces of prawn. Set aside.

Put the garlic, ground white pepper, fish sauce, soy sauce, sesame oil and palm sugar or honey into a bowl and whisk well with a fork to combine. Add the blended prawns and the pork and get in there with one hand to combine the marinade ingredients with the prawns and pork.

At this point the mixture will be quite wet. Add the cornflour (cornstarch) or tapioca flour and continue stirring until the mixture becomes drier to the touch. Mix in the chopped spring onions (scallions) and set aside for 5 minutes to allow the flour to absorb the excess moisture.

Take a wonton wrapper and place a good tablespoon of this mixture in the centre. Work the wrapper up the sides of the filling, pleating it if you can (although this isn't really necessary for delicious kanom jeeb). Leave the top open and sprinkle with the diced carrot. Repeat with the remaining wonton wrappers and filling.

Bring a saucepan of water to a boil. Place your little kanom jeeb in a steamer and set that over the pan of boiling water. I have a multi-layer steamer but you might need to do this in batches. Steam the kanom jeeb for 10 minutes.

While these are steaming, make your dipping sauce. Combine the soy sauce, dark soy sauce, sriracha sauce and vinegar in a small bowl. Taste it; some sriracha sauces are sweeter than others so add more sugar if needed or leave it as is.

Serve the kanom jeeb hot alongside the dipping sauce.

# FISHCAKES
MAKES 12

Thai fishcakes (often called 'tod mun pla' on menus) are known for their spongy consistency, which I'm not fond of; that sponginess comes from the egg, so I tend to leave it out. Fishcakes are usually deep-fried in street stalls and restaurants, but I find it much easier to shallow-fry them. These are great served with sweet chilli sauce, Thai seafood dipping sauce and/or cucumber and chilli relish (see pages 142, 144 and 145).

PREP TIME: 15 MINS
COOKING TIME: 10 MINS

500g (1lb 2oz) meaty fish fillets, such as lemon sole, cod or salmon, skinned
1 tbsp finely chopped coriander (cilantro) (optional)
1 tsp sugar (optional)
3–4 tbsp Thai red curry paste (see page 14 or 2 tbsp shop-bought paste)
1 tbsp Thai fish sauce (gluten-free brands are available)
1 tbsp lime juice
1 medium egg (optional)
1 tbsp tapioca starch
3 lime leaves, stalks removed and finely julienned
2 spring onions (scallions), thinly sliced
8 green (string) beans, thinly sliced
5 tbsp rapeseed (canola) oil

Place the fish in a food processor. Add the rest of the ingredients up to and including the lime juice. If you are using egg for a spongier fishcake, add it at this point too. Blend until you have a fine fish paste. It is worth blending for a few minutes as the heat from your blender will help thicken the paste.

Transfer to a bowl and add the tapioca starch, lime leaves, spring onions (scallions) and beans and mix well with your hand. Divide into twelve patties. I often fry a spoonful of the paste to test for seasoning, then adjust if necessary.

Heat the oil in a large, non-stick frying pan over a medium heat. Fry the fishcakes, in batches of about three or four, for about 2 minutes on one side, then flip over to cook the other side until they are nicely browned and cooked through. Each batch should only take about 4 minutes. Serve hot.

# CORN FRITTERS
MAKES SERVES 8

These corn fritters make a delicious starter or drink-time snack. You can make these with fresh or frozen corn kernels if you prefer but I use tinned for ease.

PREP TIME: 10 MINS
COOKING TIME: 10 MINS

400g (14oz) tinned (canned) sweetcorn
60g (1/2 cup) plain (all-purpose) flour
1 large egg
1 garlic clove, peeled and roughly chopped
1 tbsp Thai red curry paste (see page 14 or shop-bought)
6 tbsp thick coconut milk
2 tbsp finely chopped coriander (cilantro)
2 lime leaves, stalks removed and finely julienned
2 spring onions (scallions), finely chopped
1/4 tsp ground white pepper
Salt, to taste
Rapeseed (canola) oil, for deep-frying
Lime wedges, to serve
Sweet chilli sauce (see page 142 or shop-bought), to serve

Put two-thirds of the sweetcorn into a food processor with the flour, egg, garlic, red curry paste, coconut milk and coriander (cilantro) and blend to a smooth, thick batter. Pour this batter into a bowl and add the lime leaves, spring onions, (scallions) and remaining corn. Add the pepper and salt to taste.

Heat about 10cm (4in) of oil in a heavy-based saucepan and heat to 180°C (350°F), or when a small piece of the batter sizzles immediately when dropped into the oil. I often fry a spoonful of batter to test for seasoning, then adjust if necessary.

Take two spoons: scoop up some of the batter with one and carefully scrape the batter into the oil with the other. Repeat with the remaining batter. For best results cook these in two batches. Fry for about 3 minutes, or until the fritters turn a light brown, and then turn them over to continue frying for another couple of minutes until crispy and golden brown.

Serve hot with lime wedges and sweet chilli dipping sauce.

**Left:** Fishcakes with Thai seafood dipping sauce (page 144), sweet chilli sauce (page 142), and cucumber and chilli relish (page 145)

# PRAWN TOASTS
## SERVES 6 OR MORE

**These aren't like those you find at most takeaways: thinly layered with a bit of prawn (shrimp). No way! These are slightly larger than bite-size prawn mountains. They are amazing served with the sweet chilli sauce on page 142.**

PREP TIME: 15 MINS
COOKING TIME: 5 MINS

500g (1lb 2oz) peeled and deveined prawns (shrimp)
10 coriander (cilantro) stalks, finely chopped (about 2 generous tbsp)
6 lime leaves, de-stalked and finely chopped
4 garlic cloves, finely chopped
2 tbsp Thai fish sauce
1 egg white
½ tsp white sugar
1 French baguette, sliced into 2cm (¾in) thick slices
White or black sesame seeds, for sprinkling
Rapeseed (canola) oil, for frying

Place the prawns (shrimp) in a food processor. Add the coriander, lime leaves, garlic, fish sauce, egg white and sugar and blend to a thick paste that is somewhat gooey, like a soft dough.

Lay the bread slices on a clean work surface and top each with a generous amount of the prawn mixture. I like to pile them high like a mound – no skimping allowed! Press the prawn mounds firmly in place on each piece of bread. Sprinkle with sesame seeds. You could just sprinkle a few on or go all out and coat the whole top with them – that's up to you.

Heat about 10cm (4in) of oil in a large saucepan or wok over a medium–high heat. You are aiming for a frying temperature of 180°C (350°F). When your oil is ready, carefully place the bread, prawn-side down, in the oil and fry for 2 minutes until the prawn coating is turning a delicious light brown colour (cook in batches if necessary). Flip the toasts over and fry for another minute or so to colour the other side. Transfer with a slotted spoon to paper towels to soak up any excess oil. Serve hot.

# TEMPURA GARLIC PRAWNS
## MAKES 20

**Here is another Thai starter you might think belongs in a Japanese cookbook. However, once you try these crisp prawns (shrimp) dipped into Thai seafood dipping sauce or sweet chilli sauce, you'll find them to be 100% Thai. As in the photograph, you can fry veggies in the same way to make a tempura feast!**

PREP TIME: 20 MINS
COOKING TIME: 10 MINS

20 prawns (shrimp), peeled and deveined but tails left on
225g (scant 2 cups) sifted plain (all-purpose) flour
2 tbsp rice flour
500ml (2 cups) ice-cold sparkling water
1 egg, beaten
1 tsp salt
1 tsp garlic powder
Rapeseed (canola) oil, for deep-frying
Thai seafood dipping sauce or sweet chilli sauce (see pages 144 or 142, or shop-bought), to serve

Using a sharp knife make three shallow slits in the underside of each prawn (shrimp) and then bend it upwards to straighten. This will prevent the prawns from curling when fried, making them easier to dip into the batter and then oil.

Sift the flours into a large bowl and then stir in the sparkling water, beaten egg, salt and garlic powder and whisk it all together. Your batter will be quite runny. Heat about 10cm (4in) of the oil in a large saucepan or wok until it reaches 170–180°C (340–350°F) – or until a small bit of the batter dropped into the oil sizzles instantly.

Fry in batches of only four or five to avoid reducing the oil temperature. Hold a prawn by the tail and dip it into the batter. Shake off any excess and then slowly lower it into the hot oil. Repeat with a few more and fry for about 2 minutes, or until crispy. Drain on paper towels to soak up the excess oil and continue until all of the prawns are cooked. Serve immediately with Thai seafood dipping sauce or sweet chilli sauce.

**Top:** Prawn toasts
**Bottom:** Tempura garlic prawns and vegetables

# FIRECRACKER PRAWNS
MAKES 20

Prawns (shrimp) curl naturally into half-circles. To get your firecracker prawns looking right you need to do some cosmetic work but it's an easy job: the underside of the prawns needs to be scored in three places so that you can straighten them up. I have seen this popular starter prepared with many different marinades but as the name implies, it's the chilli that is important. In this recipe I suggest using both chilli paste and roasted chilli flakes. How much of each you add, however, is completely down to you and how spicy you like your food. I recommend serving these with sweet chilli sauce (see page 142).

PREP TIME: 20 MINS, PLUS
MARINATING TIME
COOKING TIME: 10 MINS

20 large raw prawns (shrimp), peeled and deveined but tails left on
10 egg roll wrappers
1 tsp cornflour (cornstarch)
Rapeseed (canola) oil, for deep-frying or shallow-frying

FOR THE MARINADE
1 garlic clove, finely minced
1 tsp soy sauce
1 tsp honey
1 tbsp homemade chilli jam (nam prik pao) (see page 142, or shop-bought)
1 tsp roasted chilli flakes (see page 22) (optional)
½ tsp lemon juice

Using a sharp knife, make three shallow slits in the underside of each prawn (shrimp): one at one end, then in the middle and one more at the other end. Then bend the prawn upwards to straighten. Pat the prawns dry with a paper towel. Whisk the marinade ingredients in a bowl and taste to adjust the seasoning – add the roasted chilli flakes if you want additional heat. Mix the prawns into the marinade and marinate for 30 minutes in the fridge.

Meanwhile, cut the egg roll wrappers in half diagonally, so that you get two triangles out of each square wrapper. Cover and set aside until ready to assemble. Whisk the cornflour (cornstarch) with 1 tablespoon of cold water with a fork to make a thick paste.

When you're ready to put this delicious starter together, place one of the triangle egg rolls in front of you with the long end on the left. Place one of the marinated prawns about a quarter of the way up so that the tail end is sticking over the long end of the wrapper but the head end is on the wrapper. Fold the bottom corner of the triangle over the prawn and roll it up until you reach the right corner of the triangle and fold it over so that the prawn is securely in the pastry with just the tail end visible. Brush with a little cornflour mixture to secure and then continue wrapping upwards until you have a neatly wrapped prawn. Brush again with the cornflour mixture to secure. Repeat with the remaining prawns.

To cook, either deep-fry or shallow-fry in about 2cm (1in) of oil over a medium–high heat until the wrappers are a golden brown and the prawns are cooked through. This should take about 3 minutes. Serve hot.

# SALT AND PEPPER FRIED CALAMARI
SERVES 4

My first job out of college was working as the manager of a shoe store in Marina, near Monterey, California. I hated every second of that job but loved living in Monterey and all the amazing locally caught seafood. Squid was and still is a speciality there, and it was during my time of selling cheap shoes that I learned this method of frying calamari to perfection. I've tried a few other recipes but, in my opinion, this one ticks all the boxes. The crispy fried squid is delicious served with the sweet chilli sauce dip on page 142.

PREP TIME: 5 MINS, PLUS
MARINATING TIME
COOKING TIME: 8 MINS

900g (2lb) small squid tubes and tentacles, cleaned (see note)
500ml (2 cups) full-fat (whole) milk, plus more if needed
2 eggs
6 red spur chillies, slit lengthways
120g (1 cup) plain (all-purpose) flour
120g (1 cup) cornflour (cornstarch)
1 tsp salt
1 tbsp red chilli powder
Rapeseed (canola) oil, for deep-frying
Flaky sea salt and freshly ground black pepper
Sweet chilli sauce (see page 142), to serve

Place the whole squid tubes and tentacles in a bowl and pour over 250ml (1 cup) of the milk. Milk is a natural tenderizer, which gives the squid a perfect texture when fried, so be sure the squid is completely covered; add a little more if necessary. Cover the bowl with cling film (plastic wrap) and place in the fridge overnight to marinate.

When ready to cook, drain the squid, discarding the milk, which will have turned pink due to the colouring of the tentacles. Add the remaining 250ml (1 cup) of milk to the bowl and whisk in the eggs until smooth. Return the squid to the bowl along with the spur chillies. Mix both flours together on a large plate with the salt and chilli powder.

Now heat about 750ml (3 cups) of oil in a wok and heat to 190°C (375°F) over a medium–high heat. If the oil is not hot enough, your calamari will become oily and soggy instead of deliciously crispy.

It is important to work in batches so as not to overcrowd the pan. Dip the squid and chillies into the flour mixture, ensuring each piece .is coated evenly, then fry for about 1 minute, or until golden brown. Transfer the calamari and chillies to a paper towel to soak up the excess oil and repeat until all of the squid and chillies are cooked. Season with salt and pepper to taste and serve with sweet chilli sauce.

NOTE
I purchase my squid already cleaned, which is of course the easiest option. If you can only get uncleaned squid, cleaning them isn't difficult. Pull the head from the tube body and remove and discard the long stiff cartilage from the tube. Then cut the head and ink sac away from the tentacles and discard. Peel the thin membrane from the tube and you're ready to go.

# GARLIC AND PEPPER SOFT-SHELL CRAB

SERVES 4 OR MORE

If you love garlic and crab, this is one you have to try. I first tried this at a Thai restaurant in Monterey, California back in the early nineties and went back the very next night to order the same thing! I was hoping the chef would give me his exact recipe but no such luck, so this is my interpretation of the dish. In the UK, soft-shell crab can be difficult to find, but it is available at Asian shops and some fishmongers in the freezer section. There isn't a lot of chilli in this one but it still has a good kick because of the black pepper and green peppercorns.

PREP TIME: 15 MINS
COOKING TIME: 15 MINS

Rapeseed (canola) or peanut oil,
  for shallow-frying
70g (½ cup) plain (all-purpose)
  flour
1 tsp fine sea salt
6 soft-shell crabs, completely
  defrosted and quartered
6 garlic cloves, roughly chopped
1 generous tbsp coriander
  (cilantro) stalks, finely
  chopped
¼ green (bell) pepper, cut into
  small dice
1 red spur chilli, thinly sliced
1½ tbsp fresh green peppercorns
3 spring onions (scallions),
  thinly sliced
1 tsp freshly ground black
  pepper
2 tbsp Chinese rice wine or
  dry sherry
1 tsp Thai fish sauce
1 tsp palm sugar, finely chopped
  (or use white sugar)
1 tsp garlic powder
Salt, to taste (optional)

Heat about 2.5cm (1in) of oil in a frying pan over a medium–high heat. Pour the flour and salt on a plate and mix well. Take your soft-shell crab pieces and dredge them in the flour mixture. When the oil begins to shimmer, you are ready to fry. If you want to check first, throw a piece of spring onion (scallion) in. If it sizzles immediately, you've got the perfect temperature.

Place the crabs in the oil and fry for about 2 minutes on each side, or until almost cooked through and nicely browned on the exterior. Transfer to a paper towel to soak up the excess oil and set aside.

Now heat a wok or large frying pan over a medium–high heat and add 2 tablespoons of the oil you just fried the crab in. When hot, add the garlic and coriander (cilantro) stalks and fry, stirring continuously for about 30 seconds. Be careful not to burn the garlic. Add the green (bell) pepper and red chilli. Long red chillies aren't very spicy but you could remove the seeds if you want a milder result.

Stir this all well into the oil and then add the green peppercorns, spring onions (scallions) and black pepper. Stir well to combine. Add the rice wine/sherry, fish sauce, sugar and garlic powder and again stir to combine.

Add the fried crabs and cook for a few minutes until nicely coated with the sauce ingredients and heated through. Taste and adjust the flavours and serve immediately.

# SWEET AND CRISPY CHICKEN WINGS
MAKES 12

These sweet and savoury chicken wings are a Thai restaurant and takeaway favourite. I use palm sugar when I make this recipe, but you could just use equal amounts of white granulated sugar or honey if you like. The palm sugar is more authentic and also gives a deeper colour to the dish. Although the crispy fried garlic garnish is optional, I would encourage you to take some time to make it for this recipe. I love fried garlic and it really takes this recipe up a notch or two in my opinion.

PREP TIME 10 MINS
COOKING TIME 35 MINS

12 chicken wings, bony ends cut off
3 generous tbsp black peppercorns
150g (1 cup) shallots, peeled and thinly sliced
2 tbsp finely chopped ginger
135g (⅔ cup) granulated sugar or finely chopped palm sugar
150ml (⅔ cup) Thai fish sauce*
3 spring onions (scallions), roughly chopped, to garnish
1 red spur chilli, thinly sliced, to garnish
3 tbsp crispy fried garlic (see page 148), to garnish (optional)

When you purchase whole chicken wings and lay them out, you will see that there are three parts to them: two meaty pieces and then the wing tip that has very little, if any, meat on it. Place your finger over the first joint and you will feel a small ridge. Take a sharp knife and slice through that ridge. Move to the second joint and do the same. Keep those meaty wing pieces for this recipe and use the wing tips in stocks.

Preheat the oven to 230°C (455°F/Gas 8) and line a baking tray with parchment paper.

Place the peppercorns, shallots and ginger in a pestle and mortar or food processor and pound or blend into a coarse paste. Set aside.

Put the sugar into a saucepan with 70ml (¼ cup) of water and place over a medium heat. Bring to a simmer so that the sugar dissolves into the water, and continue simmering over a low heat until the sugar is light brown in colour and beginning to caramelize and become syrupy. Be really careful not to burn the sugar or you will have to start all over again. Once you have a nice syrup, remove from the heat and very carefully add the fish sauce. Do this slowly so that it doesn't splatter when you add it.

Add the chicken and the peppercorn, ginger and shallot paste and stir well to combine. Place back over a low heat, cover the pan and simmer for 8–10 minutes, or until the chicken is cooked through. The chicken will take on the delicious golden colour of the syrup mixture.

Using tongs or a slotted spoon, transfer the chicken wings to the lined baking tray. Brush each wing with a little more of the syrup, making sure that each has a bit of the paste on top.

Bake in the oven for 10 minutes, or until the chicken is beginning to get crispy. Transfer the wings to a serving plate and drizzle with a little more of the sauce. Garnish with the spring onions, red chilli slices and crispy fried garlic (if using).

NOTE

*Many Thai fish sauces contain gluten but there are gluten-free brands available.

# FISH SAUCE AND GARLIC CHICKEN WINGS
MAKES 12

Although I have had whole chicken wings served to me at a few restaurants, I recommend trimming off the ends and only using the fat, meaty bit in the middle – you can always use the unused parts in a good Thai chicken stock (see page 18). Many people love Thai chicken wings with a sweet chilli dipping sauce (see page 142); for me, however, it has to be nam jim jaew (see page 144)! We served it with both in this picture.

PREP TIME: 10 MINS
COOKING TIME: 10 MINS

12 chicken wings, bony ends cut off
4 tbsp Thai fish sauce
½ tsp ground white pepper
120g (1 cup) plain (all-purpose) flour or fine rice flour (to make this gluten-free)
1 tsp chilli powder
1 tbsp garlic powder
Rapeseed (canola) oil, for deep-frying
Your choice of dipping sauce, to serve

When you purchase whole chicken wings and lay them out, you will see that there are three parts to them. Two meaty pieces and then the wing tip that has very little, if any, meat on it. Place your finger over the first joint and you will feel a small ridge. Take a sharp knife and slice through that ridge. Move to the second joint and do the same. Keep those meaty wing pieces for this recipe and use the wing tips in stocks.

Put the chicken wing pieces into a bowl and pour the fish sauce all over them. Add the white pepper and mix well with your hands so that they are completely covered in the marinade. Set aside. Pour the flour, chilli powder and garlic powder onto a plate and mix well. Set aside.

Now heat about 750ml (3 cups) of oil in a large saucepan or wok until it reaches 175°C (350°F). If you don't have a thermometer, your oil is ready when a small piece of chicken placed in the hot oil sizzles immediately.

When your oil is ready, take the chicken wings and roll them in the flour mixture so that they are really well dusted with the flour. Carefully lower them into the oil. You might want to do this in batches so that you don't overcrowd the pan and cool the oil down. Fry for 8–10 minutes, or until golden brown and cooked through. Transfer to paper towels to soak up any excess oil. Let them rest for about 5 minutes and the skin will become even crispier.

Serve hot with the dipping sauce of your choice.

NOTE
*Many Thai fish sauces contain gluten but gluten-free brands are available.

# CHICKEN SATAY WITH PEANUT SAUCE
SERVES 6

I'm a big fan of Thai chicken satay with peanut sauce. Although it isn't necessary, it is best to marinate the chicken for at least a day. You could get away with 30 minutes but a longer marinating time will get you much tastier results. As the chicken soaks up that incredible marinade, it not only tenderizes it but makes it much juicier when cooked. This recipe could be used with thinly sliced pork or beef – both are also popular at Thai restaurants and takeaways. Pork is the meat of choice in Thailand but chicken is the most popular in the UK. I also like to serve this dish with cucumber and chilli relish (see page 145).

PREP TIME: 20 MINS
COOKING TIME: 15 MINS

1kg (2lb 2oz) skinless chicken breast or thigh fillets, cut into bite-size pieces

FOR THE MARINADE
1 tbsp cumin seeds
1 tbsp coriander seeds
½ tsp ground white pepper
2 tsp ground turmeric
4 lime leaves, stalks removed and leaves finely chopped
1 tbsp thinly sliced lemongrass
1 generous tbsp chopped galangal
200ml (generous ¾ cup) coconut milk
A pinch of ground cinnamon
2 tsp palm or white sugar
1 tbsp white wine or rice vinegar
1 tsp salt

FOR THE PEANUT SAUCE
1 tbsp rapeseed (canola) oil
2 tbsp Thai red curry paste (see page 14 or shop-bought to taste)
400ml (1¾ cups) thick coconut milk
200ml (generous ¾ cup) smooth or chunky peanut butter
2 tbsp Thai fish sauce* (or more to taste)
1 tbsp sugar (or more to taste)
Juice of 1 lime
2 tbsp tamarind water (see page 17, or use more lime juice)

To make the marinade, toast the cumin and coriander seeds over a medium heat in a dry frying pan until warm to the touch and fragrant but not yet smoking. Transfer to a pestle and mortar and grind to a smooth powder. Add the ground white pepper and turmeric.

Now add the lime leaves, lemongrass and galangal to the mortar and pound with the cumin, coriander and pepper into a fine paste. Add the coconut milk, cinnamon, sugar, vinegar and salt and stir well to combine.

Put the chicken into a bowl and pour the marinade over it. Work the marinade into the meat with one of your hands so it is very well coated. Set aside. For best results, marinate overnight but this isn't necessary.

Now make the peanut sauce. Heat the oil in a large pan over a medium heat and add the red curry paste. Stir it around in the oil for about 30 seconds. Add the coconut milk followed by the peanut butter and stir to combine until the peanut butter melts into the coconut milk. Stir in the fish sauce and sugar and check for seasoning, adding more fish sauce and/or sugar if you prefer a saltier/sweeter flavour. Finish the sauce by adding the lime juice and tamarind water. It will thicken as it cools; to thin it out again, just heat it up.

Now to cook the chicken. Soak wooden skewers in water for about 30 minutes. Then skewer the meat onto each skewer.

I prefer to cook these on the barbecue but a griddle (grill) pan will do fine if you would rather cook indoors. For the barbecue, build a fire in one half of the barbecue and leave the other half without any coals. This way, you can cook the chicken over the heat without burning the skewers. If cooking indoors on a griddle pan, lightly grease the pan with oil and cook over a medium–high heat on one side for about 5 minutes before flipping the skewers over to cook the other side. Continue turning until the chicken is cooked through and you are happy with the appearance. Serve with warmed peanut sauce.

NOTE
*Most fish sauces contain gluten but gluten-free brands are available.

# FRIED CRISPY DUCK
SERVES 4–6

Crispy duck might be Chinese in origin but it is on so many Thai menus that I just had to include it in this book. You need to allow yourself a good couple of days to get this one right, but the actual work involved is minimal. You will need a large enough steamer to hold the duck. Large bamboo steamers that sit over a wok are not expensive but any large steamer will do. It is perfectly fine to cut the duck lengthwise down the centre into two halves if you don't have a large enough steamer or wok to steam/ fry a whole duck. I do this often. This fried crispy duck is often served wrapped in Mandarin pancakes (see page 21) with strips of spring onion, cucumber and Chinese plum sauce. I usually skip the sweet plum sauce and top mine with nam jim jaew (see page 144), chilli jam (page 142) or sriracha sauce (see page 145) instead. It is pictured here with nam jim jaew and chilli jam.

PREP TIME: 25 MINS,
PLUS MARINATING AND
CHILLING TIME
COOKING TIME: 1 HOUR
40 MINS

1 Gressingham duck, tail cut off
2 tbsp salt
3 tbsp Szechuan peppercorns
4 spring onions (scallions),
   sliced lengthwise
1 thumb-sized piece of galangal,
   thinly sliced into about
   8 rounds
3 tbsp Chinese rice wine or
   dry sherry
1 litre (4 cups) rapeseed (canola)
   oil, for deep-frying
2 tbsp cornflour (cornstarch)

The first step is optional but produces a deliciously crispy skin. Carefully stick a finger or two under the skin and move it around to separate the skin from the meat. You will need to do this from several different angles.

The second step is essential. Press down on the duck hard to flatten it and give it a nice massage, pushing down on the legs, breasts and back until quite limp and broken but still whole.

Heat a frying pan over a medium heat and toast the salt and Szechuan peppercorns for about a minute until fragrant. Place the duck in a glass or ceramic tray and pour this mixture all over the duck. Rub it right into the skin and then rub the spring onions (scallions) and galangal in too, so that it picks up the flavour of their juices. Put the galangal and spring onions into the carcass and then rub the Chinese rice wine or sherry into the skin. Place in the fridge overnight, uncovered, to marinate and dry out.

The next day, place the duck in a large steamer and steam over a medium–high heat for 1½ hours. Put the steamed duck back into the fridge, uncovered, for 24 hours or up to 48 hours. This will help the skin dry.

When ready to fry, heat the oil in a large wok or deep saucepan until it reaches between 160–180°C (320–350°F). Rub the duck all over with the cornflour (cornstarch). This will make the fried skin extra crispy. Carefully lower the duck into the hot oil and fry for about 10 minutes, or until golden brown. Transfer to a chopping board and let it rest for about 5 minutes.

Carve at the table to serve in pancakes as mentioned above, or cut it into small pieces for use in a curry such as red duck curry (see page 107).

# GARLICKY SALT AND PEPPER PORK RIBS
SERVES 2–4

These ribs are comfort food at its best and a moreish way to start a delicious Thai meal. I like to serve them with nam jim jaew (see page 144) or sweet chilli sauce (see page 142).

PREP TIME: 10 MINS, PLUS OPTIONAL MARINATING TIME
COOKING TIME: 20 MINS

125ml (½ cup) rice wine vinegar
2 tbsp light soy sauce (gluten-free brands are available)
1 tbsp oyster sauce (gluten-free brands are available)
1 tsp roasted chilli flakes (see page 22)
6 garlic cloves, minced
2 tsp freshly ground black pepper
2 tsp salt
1 rack of pork baby back ribs, cut into small 2.5cm (1in) pieces
7 tbsp cornflour (cornstarch)
Rapeseed (canola) oil, for deep-frying
Your choice of dipping sauce

Put all the ingredients up to and including the salt in a bowl and whisk together. Taste and adjust the ingredients to your preferences.

Add the pork ribs and mix well with your hands to combine. Although you could fry these immediately, leaving them to marinate for a few hours or overnight will improve the flavour.

Just before you are ready to cook, add the cornflour (cornstarch) to the bowl and mix well to ensure the ribs are equally coated all over.

Pour about 5cm (2in) rapeseed (canola) oil into a wok or frying pan. Heat to about 160°C (320°F). You need to fry the pork for about 20 minutes, so it is important not to let it get too hot. When hot, add the pork to the oil and fry for 15–20 minutes, depending on how meaty your ribs are. The meat should turn a crispy brown and be really tender. When frying like this, use your eyes! If the meat looks like it is burning, remove it from the oil.

Transfer to a plate lined with paper towels to soak up any excess oil. Serve immediately with the dipping sauce of your choice.

# PORK MEATBALLS
MAKES 20

These meatballs are packed with delicious flavours. I like to serve them with a couple of dips like sweet chilli sauce and chilli jam (see page 142). Before cooking them, I recommend frying up a bit of the prepared meat and adjusting the flavour to taste.

PREP TIME: 10 MINS
COOKING TIME: 10 MINS

1 lemongrass stalk (white part only), bruised and cut into rings
5 spring onions (scallions), finely chopped
4 garlic cloves, finely chopped
2.5cm (1in) piece of galangal, finely chopped
3 red bird's eye chillies, finely chopped
3 lime leaves, stalks removed and leaves finely chopped
1 tsp clear honey or grated palm sugar
2 tbsp Thai fish sauce (gluten-free brands are available)
30g (1 cup) fresh coriander (cilantro), finely chopped
500g (1lb) minced (ground) pork
3 tbsp rapeseed (canola) oil
Lime wedges, to serve (optional)

Place the lemongrass in a pestle and mortar and pound to a fine paste. Add the spring onions (scallions), garlic, galangal, chillies and lime leaves and pound until you have a nice paste and the ingredients are thoroughly combined. This should only take about 5 minutes. Transfer to a bowl and add the honey or palm sugar, fish sauce, coriander (cilantro) and pork, then mix this all up with your hands. For a finer finish, you can blend this mixture in a food processor.

Form into about twenty balls roughly 3.75cm (1½in) in diameter. At this point you could use them in a soup by simmering them in the broth.

To serve as a starter, heat the oil in a frying pan over a medium heat. When hot, add the meatballs and brown them all over, moving them around the pan regularly. After about 3–5 minutes they should be nicely browned and cooked through. Serve immediately with a squeeze of lime juice if desired.

# EASY NORTHERN PORK SAUSAGE PATTIES
MAKES 8

I make Thai sausages all the time. They are really good and delicious served in so many ways. Officially speaking, these aren't northern Thai sausages at all; the real thing would be stuffed into sausage casings and hung for a few days in the air to ferment. I know that most people don't have sausage machines at home (I do have one; the question is where I put it about 10 years ago) so I came up with this simpler version. Obviously, if you have a sausage machine and can pick up casings from a good butcher, you could use this recipe to make more authentic Thai sausages. These are great with sweet chilli sauce (see page 142) but you could also try these with nam jim jaew or chilli jam (pages 144 and 142).

PREP TIME: 5 MINS
COOKING TIME: 10 MINS

450g (1lb) minced (ground) pork
2–3 tbsp Thai red curry paste (see page 14 or shop-bought to taste)
1 tbsp rapeseed (canola) oil
Sweet chilli sauce (see page 142 or shop-bought), to serve

Mix the pork with the Thai red curry paste. While doing this, squeeze the meat with your hands – this will break it down a little and also ensure the meat is thoroughly coated with the curry paste. If you are unsure about the spiciness and saltiness of the curry paste you are using, try some. The first time you make this recipe, it is a good idea to check the seasoning by cooking a small amount. Divide the meat into eight small patties.

Pour the oil into a frying pan over a medium–high heat. When hot, add the pork patties and fry for about 3 minutes on each side.

Check they are thoroughly cooked and serve hot with sweet chilli sauce.

# THAI-STYLE CHILLI GARLIC EDAMAME
SERVES 4 AS A STARTER

I'm always happy when I go out for a Thai meal and I see edamame on the menu as a starter. It might be a very simple dish to make but it's so addictive. I just can't get enough and the great thing is you can make it at home with equally delicious results. You will find bags of frozen edamame in pods at most Asian grocers and they are also found in the freezer section of many supermarkets. The pods aren't eaten but it is important to buy the edamame in the pod so you can pick them up and scrape the beans and all that amazing flavour stuck to the pod straight into your mouth.

PREP TIME: 5 MINS
COOKING TIME: 10 MINS

500g (1lb 2oz) edamame beans in the pod
3 garlic cloves, finely chopped
1½ tsp rapeseed (canola) oil
1 tbsp sesame oil
1 tbsp red chilli flakes
1 tbsp light soy sauce*
Flaky sea salt, to taste

Bring a saucepan of water to a boil. Add the edamame and simmer over a medium heat for 3 minutes, then drain and keep warm.

Whisk together the garlic, both oils, chilli flakes and soy sauce in a serving bowl. Feel free at this point to adjust the flavour of the marinade by adding more chilli flakes, for example. Add the hot edamame and stir well to combine. Season with flaky salt to taste and serve immediately.

NOTE
*Many soy sauces contain gluten but gluten-free brands are available.

# SALADS AND SOUPS

Salads and soups are the perfect way to start a Thai
feast. In this section you will find the most popular salads
and soups served at Thai restaurants and takeaways.
Make them as I've written them here or have some fun
experimenting. You could add rice or wheat noodles to the
soups, for example, to make them more filling as a main
dish. Another nice addition is fish balls (see page 19) as
well as pork meatballs (see page 51) that you can add raw
and simmer in the soups until cooked through.

# GREEN PAPAYA SALAD
SERVES 4

Almost every Thai restaurant and takeaway has this famous salad on the menu. The Thai name for this salad is som tum (sour pounded). There are hundreds of 'tum' salads in Thailand but this seems to be the one that people outside of Thailand know and love most. The dressing ingredients are pounded with a pestle and mortar and then mixed into the crispy fruit and vegetables, offering the perfect combination of sour, sweet, savoury and spicy. Som tum salads are like Thai coleslaw – they won't wilt so you can make this in advance and bring it out, cold from the fridge, to serve. Green papaya can be found a large supermarkets and Asian grocers. The idea behind this recipe is to achieve a pounded dressing that is like a paste. If you don't have a pestle and mortar, you can cheat with a food processor.

**PREP TIME: 15 MINS**
**COOKING TIME: 5 MINS**

2 tbsp peanuts (raw or roasted)
1½ tbsp dried baby shrimp
3 garlic cloves
2–3 red bird's eye chillies
12 green (string) beans, cut into
    2.5cm (1in) pieces
1 tbsp palm sugar, grated and
    finely chopped
1 tbsp tamarind paste (see page
    17 or shop-bought)
2 tbsp Thai fish sauce*
Juice of 1 large lime
400g (14oz) green papaya, grated
1 medium carrot, peeled and
    grated
6 baby plum tomatoes, halved
2 tbsp finely chopped coriander
    (cilantro)
2 tbsp Thai sweet basil (or any
    basil), roughly chopped

Place the peanuts in a pestle and mortar and pound lightly to break them up a little – just a bit! Tip the peanuts into a frying pan and roast over a medium–high heat until fragrant and roasted to a light brown. If you're using shop-bought roasted peanuts, you can of course skip this step. Pour the peanuts into a bowl and set aside.

Now put the dried baby shrimp into your pestle and mortar and pound away until they are broken up into a coarse paste. Then add the garlic and bird's eye chillies and continue pounding them into the shrimp. This is not a fine paste. You should still be able to see small pieces of the individual ingredients among the paste. Add the green (string) beans and pound some more, crushing and bruising them (but they should still look like pieces of green bean). Add the sugar, tamarind paste, fish sauce and lime juice and stir this all up well with your pestle, pressing all the ingredients into the base of your mortar. It is important that the sugar gets completely dissolved into the dressing. Check for seasoning, adding more lime juice for sourness, sugar for sweetness, chillies if you prefer a spicier dressing and/or fish sauce for a saltier flavour.

Put your grated green papaya and carrot into a salad bowl and pour the dressing all over it. Stir well to combine so that the grated papaya and carrot are well coated with the dressing. Add the halved plum tomatoes, roasted peanuts, coriander and basil and again, stir well. For best results, chill in the fridge before serving, although sometimes I honestly can't wait that long.

NOTE
*Many Thai fish sauces contain gluten but there are gluten-free brands available.

MAKE IT VEGETARIAN / VEGAN
Simply leave out the baby shrimp to make this a tasty vegan salad.

# TURKEY LARB SALAD
SERVES 4

I felt it was a good idea to feature this salad, not just because it's really good and light, but because it demonstrates another popular way to serve larb. Pork larb is by far the most popular but you could make it with other ingredients such as minced (ground) turkey, chicken or beef. Here I decided to use finely chopped turkey breast instead of minced to show another way larb can be cooked and presented. The salad dressing and salad ingredients are also good tossed with slices of weeping tiger steak (see page 122) to make a weeping tiger beef salad.

PREP TIME: 15 MINS
COOKING TIME: 15 MINS

FOR THE DRESSING
Juice of 2 limes (about 70ml/
¼ cup)
1 tbsp rapeseed (canola) oil
1 tbsp finely grated palm sugar
or honey
3 garlic cloves, finely chopped
1 red spur chilli, thinly sliced and
seeds removed for a milder
dressing
10 mint leaves, finely chopped
½ cucumber, thinly sliced

FOR THE LARB
2 tbsp rapeseed (canola) oil
450g (1lb) turkey breasts,
finely chopped
4 shallots, thinly sliced
1 tbsp roasted chilli flakes (see
page 22)
1 tbsp soy sauce*
1 tbsp Thai fish sauce*
1 tbsp palm sugar or white
caster sugar
1½ tbsp roasted and ground rice
(see page 22)
4 spring onions (scallions),
roughly chopped
1–2 tbsp lime juice

FOR THE SALAD
4 large handfuls of salad greens,
such as butter lettuce, rocket
(arugula), radishes, chopped
red onion

Whisk all the dressing ingredients together and put into the fridge, covered, to chill.

Heat the oil in a large pan or wok over a medium–high heat. When hot, add the chopped turkey and fry for about 8 minutes until cooked through. Add the sliced shallots and roasted chilli flakes and stir well to combine. Now add the soy sauce, fish sauce, sugar and roasted and ground rice and stir again. Taste and adjust the flavours, adding more fish or soy sauce for more salt, sugar for sweetness and/or chilli flakes for a spicier flavour.

Stir in the chopped spring onions (scallions) and squeeze over lime juice to taste. This can be served on the salad either warm or at room temperature.

To serve, toss the salad greens with the dressing and divide between four plates. Top each with a generous mound of the turkey larb.

NOTE
*Many soy and Thai fish sauces contain gluten but gluten-free brands are available.

# GLASS NOODLE SALAD
SERVES 2

This recipe takes me back to my early twenties, dining outdoors at a Thai restaurant my friends and I used to frequent, ordering up a selection of dishes and drinking copious amounts of alcohol. Those were the days. In the hot California heat, spicy salads like this yum woon sen, or glass noodle salad, always went down a treat. These days, when the weather's nice and I'm cooking up a family Thai barbecue, this salad is always on the dinner table. It can be and often is served at room temperature, but I prefer to serve it while the pork, prawns (shrimp) and noodles are still hot.

PREP TIME: 15 MINS
COOKING TIME: 15 MINS

100g (3½oz) raw glass noodles
6 baby plum tomatoes, quartered
4 shallots, thinly sliced
1 stick celery with leaves,
    thinly sliced
10 small (or a few large) raw
    prawns (shrimp), peeled
    and deveined
125g (4½oz) minced (ground)
    pork
10 roasted cashews, roughly
    chopped
3 tbsp roughly chopped
    coriander (cilantro) leaves

FOR THE DRESSING
1 tbsp dried shrimp, soaked in
    warm water for 10 minutes
3 garlic cloves, smashed
2 tbsp finely chopped coriander
    (cilantro) stalks
3 red bird's eye chillies, roughly
    chopped
1 tbsp palm sugar, grated
3 tbsp Thai fish sauce
3½ tbsp lime juice

Soak the noodles as per the instructions on the packet, but as a rule of thumb, soak them in warm water for about 10 minutes until soft.

Meanwhile, make the dressing: place the soaked dried shrimp, garlic, coriander (cilantro) stalks, bird's eye chillies and palm sugar in a pestle and mortar and pound to a smooth paste. This should only take a minute or two. Pour in the fish sauce and lime juice and stir well. Taste and adjust the ingredients to your liking and set this dressing aside.

Put the tomatoes, shallots and celery in a salad bowl. Now bring a saucepan of water to a boil over a medium–high heat and add the soaked glass noodles to cook for about 2 minutes. Remove the noodles with tongs or a slotted spoon and place in a sieve to drain away the excess water. Set aside.

Pour out all but 125ml (½ cup) of the water in the pan and return to the heat. Add the prawns (shrimp) and cook them for about 2 minutes, or until cooked through. Transfer with a slotted spoon to rest on the hot noodles.

Add the minced (ground) pork to the remaining water and turn the heat up to high. Stir continuously, breaking the pork up as you do into the water. Cook until the water has dissolved and the pork is cooked through. This should take about 5 minutes.

Put the prawns on top of the salad vegetables and add the cooked pork to the bowl too. Top with the cooked glass noodles and then pour the dressing all over the noodles. This will help separate them. Add the chopped roasted cashews and coriander leaves and stir it all up. Serve immediately or place in the fridge to cool for about 30 minutes.

# TOM YUM GAI SOUP (HOT AND SOUR CHICKEN SOUP)
## SERVES 4–6

When you go out for Thai food this is sure to be on the menu. I love the spiciness of this soup – you get a good hit of spice but it doesn't linger. Some chefs add sugar to it but, for me, this is a spicy, savoury and tart soup with only a hint of natural sweetness from the fried shallots and tomatoes. Do, of course, taste the soup and adjust the flavour to your liking, adding sugar if you want. It makes a delicious starter but you could bulk it up by adding other ingredients such as noodles to make it a light main. The word 'gai' means chicken, so this is a chicken tom yum soup. You could substitute prawn (shrimp) stock (see page 18) and prawns to make a delicious tom yum goong, or go vegetarian and use water and tofu.

PREP TIME: 10 MINS
COOKING TIME: 20 MINS

2 tbsp rapeseed (canola) oil
2 shallots, finely chopped
1 litre (4 cups) Thai chicken
   stock (see page 18) or water
1 lemongrass stalk, smashed and
   cut into about 5 pieces
8 lime leaves, stalks removed
   and leaves thinly sliced
2.5cm (1in) piece of galangal,
   thinly sliced
3 garlic cloves, roughly chopped
250g (9oz) chicken breast, cut
   into bite-size pieces
1 tbsp tamarind paste (see page
   17 or shop-bought)
8 mushrooms, quartered
1 tbsp chilli jam (nam prik pao)
   (see page 142 or shop-bought)
1 tbsp roasted Thai chilli oil with
   some of the goop at the
   bottom (see page 146 or
   shop-bought – preferably
   Thai but Chinese is fine)
3–4 tbsp Thai fish sauce*
3 green bird's eye chillies,
   smashed and cut lengthwise
1 small handful of coriander
   (cilantro), roughly chopped
2 tsp palm or white sugar
   (optional and to taste)
2 tomatoes, quartered
3 spring onions (scallions),
   roughly chopped
Handful of chopped or sliced
   vegetables, such as cabbage,
   bean sprouts, carrots (optional)

Heat the oil in a large saucepan over a medium–high heat until shimmering hot. Add the shallots and fry for about a minute. Then add the stock or water, lemongrass, lime leaves, galangal and garlic and bring to a boil. Reduce the heat and simmer this aromatic liquid for about 10 minutes.

Now stir in the chicken and continue cooking until the chicken is cooked through. This should take about 5 minutes. Add the tamarind paste and stir well.

Stir in the mushrooms, chilli jam, chilli oil, fish sauce, green bird's eye chillies and coriander (cilantro). If you are at all worried about adding too much of any ingredient, taste as you go!

Once all of these ingredients have been added, taste it again and adjust the seasoning as desired. At this stage, you could also add a little sugar if you want it sweeter.

To finish, add the quartered tomatoes and let them cook through in the hot stock. Add the spring onions (scallions) and any other vegetables you would like to add. I often add bean sprouts, cabbage and carrots but this is totally optional – add whichever veggies you like.

To serve, ladle the soup into bowls and enjoy.

NOTE
*Many Thai fish sauces contain gluten but there are gluten-free brands available.

# TOM KHA GAI SOUP (CHICKEN, GALANGAL AND COCONUT SOUP)
SERVES 4–6

Tom kha gai is a popular spicy coconut soup. The tasty broth is more important than what you put into it as a main ingredient, which in this case is chicken, although you could substitute prawns (shrimp) to make tom kha goong, or meaty white fish. You could also leave the meat out and make it into a vegan soup, adding whichever vegetable you like or even fried tofu (see page 30). If you want to have this as a main dish, you could add other ingredients such as noodles to make the soup more filling.

PREP TIME: 10 MINS
COOKING TIME: 20 MINS

500ml (2 cups) water or Thai chicken stock (see page 18)
1 stalk lemongrass (white part only with thick outer layer removed), bruised and cut into about 6 slices
3 lime leaves, stalks removed and leaves thinly sliced
1 thumb-sized piece of galangal, bruised and sliced into 7 pieces
10 coriander (cilantro) stalks, finely chopped
250g (9oz) skinless chicken thigh fillets, cut into bite-size pieces
400ml (1¾ cups) tinned (canned) thick coconut milk
2 tbsp palm sugar (or to taste)
8 mushrooms, quartered or halved
70ml (¼ cup) Thai fish sauce*
2 tbsp roasted Thai chilli oil with some of the goop at the bottom (see page 146 or shop-bought – preferably Thai but Chinese is fine), or Thai red curry paste (see page 14 or shop-bought) to taste
80ml (⅓ cup) lime juice
3 spring onions (scallions), roughly chopped

Pour the stock into a large saucepan and bring to a boil over a high heat. Add the lemongrass, lime leaves, galangal and coriander (cilantro) stalks. Let this simmer for about 10 minutes to allow the aromatic ingredients to flavour the stock.

Add the chicken and simmer for about 5 minutes, or until the chicken is just cooked through. Pour in the coconut milk and add sugar to taste.

Now add the mushrooms, fish sauce and the chilli oil along with some of the goop at the bottom – this is usually made up of chilli flakes and perhaps garlic or shallots. You could also just add Thai red curry paste if that is more convenient. Keep tasting as you go.

Finally add the lime juice to taste and the chopped spring onions (scallions). Simmer for another minute or so and then ladle into bowls and enjoy.

NOTE

*Many Thai fish sauces contain gluten but there are gluten-free brands available.

# THAI SPICED WONTON SOUP
SERVES 4

This is that clear beef broth wonton soup you find at Chinese and Thai restaurants and takeaways. It looks so good and inviting. The most time-consuming part is preparing the clear beef broth, but I have given my no-fail method on page 19. It's better than any clear stock you can purchase but if spending 6 hours making a clear stock doesn't appeal to you, you could purchase some clear beef stock (not stock cubes) and simmer it with lemongrass and galangal. Remember, however, that most commercially available stocks have salt in them, so you might need to adjust how much soy sauce and fish sauce you add to this recipe.

PREP TIME: 20 MINS, PLUS THE TIME IT TAKES TO MAKE THE WONTON FILLING
COOKING TIME: 10 MINS

20 wonton wrappers
½ batch of kanom jeeb filling (see page 33)
1 litre (4 cups) clear Thai beef broth (see page 19)
1 tbsp Thai fish sauce
1 tbsp light soy sauce
1 tsp sugar
1 tbsp Chinese rice wine or dry sherry
3 small red bird's eye chillies, thinly sliced
3 spring onions (scallions)
8 sprigs of coriander (cilantro), to garnish

First prepare your wontons. Take one of the wonton wrappers and place it in front of you with one of the corners pointing at you. Place about a tablespoon of the filling in the centre and bring the point nearest you up and fold it over the filling to meet the point at the top. Press down hard to close the seam. Now take the right and left corners and bring them together around the filling and again press hard so that the filling is securely wrapped without any gaps. Repeat with the remain wrappers and filling, cover and set aside.

Pour the beef broth into a saucepan and add the fish sauce, soy sauce, sugar and rice wine or sherry and bring to a simmer. Add the red chillies and spring onions (scallions), turn off the heat and keep hot. Taste and adjust the flavours to your personal taste.

Bring a saucepan of water to a boil. When boiling, add the wontons and cook for 2 minutes (you don't want to do this in the beef broth as it will make it cloudy). Divide the cooked wontons between four soup bowls and pour the hot beef broth over them. Garnish with sprigs of coriander (cilantro) and serve immediately.

TIP
Whenever you make wontons, it is worth making more than you need. They freeze really well for up to 2 months. Defrost and use in soups like this.

# SEAFOOD STEW
SERVES 4

Thai seafood stew, or poh tak, is a delicious seafood soup that is often served as a starter. I like to serve it as a main course too, with a nice variety of fresh seafood and some jasmine rice or sticky rice on the side. It is hot and sour like a tom yum soup. In fact, it is the same as a tom yum soup but without the chilli paste and chilli oil, which give tom yum soups a bit more kick and their characteristic red glow. So this recipe is more about the delicious seafood than the spicy chillies, though it has a delicious spiciness to it too. If you would like to make a tom yum goong soup, just follow my tom yum gai recipe (see page 61) and add prawns (shrimp) at the end of cooking instead of chicken. You are not limited to the amount of seafood called for below. Add more seafood and perhaps a bit more stock as you see fit.

PREP TIME 15 MINS
COOKING TIME 15 MINS

2 tbsp rapeseed (canola) oil
2 shallots, finely chopped
1 litre (4 cups) Thai chicken stock or prawn stock (see page 18)
1 lemongrass stalk, smashed and cut into about 5 pieces
8 lime leaves, stalks removed and leaves thinly sliced
2.5cm (1in) piece of galangal, thinly sliced
3 garlic cloves, roughly chopped
8 mushrooms, quartered
1 tbsp tamarind paste (see page 17 or shop-bought)
3 green bird's eye chillies, smashed and cut lengthwise
1 small handful of coriander (cilantro), roughly chopped
2 tsp palm or white sugar (optional and to taste)
250g (9oz) fresh seafood, such as prawns (shrimp), mussels, clams, sea bass, halibut, crab claws, homemade fish balls (see page 19), cooked lobster
3–4 tbsp Thai fish sauce*
3 spring onions (scallions), roughly chopped
2 tomatoes, quartered

In a large saucepan that is big enough to hold the liquid and seafood of your choice, fry the shallots over a medium–high heat in the oil until soft and light brown. Pour in the stock and bring to a simmer with the lemongrass, lime leaves, galangal, and garlic. Simmer gently for 15–20 minutes. Stir in the mushrooms, tamarind paste, chillies, coriander (cilantro) and sugar.

Now think before you add your seafood. Most seafood will cook quite quickly in the simmering stock. Mussels, prawns (shrimp) and sea bass will only take a couple of minutes and you need to be very careful not to overcook seafood. Prawns, for example, will get tough if overcooked as will cooked lobster, and sea bass will flake away into the sauce, while large chunks of halibut will take longer to cook. Add your seafood in order of how quickly they cook to perfection and keep a careful eye on everything.

To finish, stir in the fish sauce and check for seasoning, adding more sugar for a sweeter flavour or stock to make it more savoury. Stir in the spring onions (scallions) and quartered tomatoes and serve.

NOTE

*Many Thai fish sauces contain gluten but there are gluten-free brands available.

# CLASSIC CURRIES

The following curries needed a chapter to themselves!
These are the curries almost everyone looks for when
they go out for Thai food. If you put in the time to make
your own curry pastes, as featured on pages 14–17, you
will be amazed at just how good these curries can be. They
can be made with shop-bought pastes if you prefer but it is
crucial that you add the pastes to taste, as many contain a
lot of salt. I would usually use half as much shop-bought
paste as homemade paste.

Although I have given popular main ingredient options
for these curries, feel free to use other ingredients such
as prawns (shrimp), duck, pork, squash and firm tofu.

# THAI GREEN CHICKEN CURRY
SERVES 4

Although many people believe that Thai red curries are the spiciest, green curries are actually spicier because of the large amount of green bird's eye chillies used in the paste. Of course, how spicy you make yours is up to you. I recommend making the Thai green curry paste on page 14 for this recipe as it is packed with delicious fresh flavours. If you want to cheat, purchase a good-quality green curry paste but reduce the quantity, as commercial pastes are usually spicier and saltier than homemade ones.

PREP TIME: 10 MINS
COOK TIME: 20 MINS

2 tbsp coconut oil or rapeseed (canola) oil
1 batch of Thai green curry paste (see page 14 or shop-bought to taste)
450g (1lb) skinless chicken thigh or breast fillets, cut into bite-size pieces
250ml (1 cup) Thai chicken stock (see page 18)
400ml (1¾ cups) thick coconut milk
About 225g (8oz) vegetables, such as baby corn, bamboo shoots, aubergine (eggplant), broccoli, sliced lotus root
2 tbsp sugar (more or less to taste)
3 tbsp Thai fish sauce*
Handful of Thai sweet basil, roughly chopped
3 lime leaves, stalks removed and leaves finely julienned
2 red spur chillies, cut into thin rings, to garnish
Basil oil and some of the goop from the bottom, to garnish (see page 146) (optional)

Heat a large wok or frying pan over a medium–high heat and add the oil. When visibly hot, add the green curry paste and fry for about 30 seconds in the oil. Add the chicken pieces and cook for a couple of minutes, stirring to combine with the paste.

Add the stock and coconut milk and bring to a simmer. Cook for about 10 minutes, or until the chicken is cooked through and the sauce thickens a little. Stir in your vegetables and cook them through to your liking. I prefer mine to be on the crunchy side and not at all mushy. Stir in the sugar, fish sauce, basil and lime leaves. Taste the curry and adjust the flavours to your preference.

Garnish with the sliced spur chillies and basil oil, if using. In the photo opposite I added 3 tablespoons of the thick basil oil. You could strain the oil and just garnish with a few drops of clear basil oil but I like to add the oil without running it through a sieve and cheesecloth.

NOTE
*Many Thai fish sauces contain gluten but there are gluten-free brands available.

# THAI RED CHICKEN CURRY
SERVES 4

This curry recipe is a Thai restaurant and takeaway favourite. The red colour comes from the curry paste and it will vary depending on how many red spur chillies you used in the paste. You can use shop-bought red curry paste but you will need to add less to begin with, as commercial pastes are often a lot spicier and saltier than homemade. One eye-catching way of adding colour to the curry is to drizzle it with red chilli oil, but this is optional.

PREP TIME: 10 MINS
COOK TIME: 20 MINS

2 tbsp coconut oil or rapeseed (canola) oil
1 batch of Thai red curry paste (see page 14 or use 2–3 tbsp shop-bought)
450g (1lb) skinless chicken thigh fillets, cut into bite-size pieces
250ml (1 cup) Thai chicken stock (see page 18)
400ml (1¾ cups) thick coconut milk
About 225g (8oz) vegetables, such as baby aubergine (eggplant), sliced red (bell) pepper, green (string) beans
3 tbsp Thai fish sauce*
1 tbsp light soy sauce*
1 tsp tamarind paste (see page 17 or shop-bought)
1 tbsp palm sugar
Coriander (cilantro) leaves, to garnish
1 tsp roasted Thai chilli oil (see page 146 or shop-bought – preferably Thai but Chinese is fine), to garnish (optional)

Heat the oil over a medium–high heat in a large frying pan or wok. When visibly hot, add the red curry paste and fry for about 30 seconds in the oil. Stir in the chicken and fry for a couple minutes, or until the chicken is about 50% cooked through. Stir in the stock and coconut milk and simmer for 5 minutes to thicken the sauce a little.

Now add the veggies, fish sauce, soy sauce, tamarind and palm sugar and simmer for about 3 minutes to cook the vegetables through. Taste and adjust the flavours as necessary, then cook the sauce down until you are happy with the consistency. It should be quite thin. Be careful not to overcook the vegetables. Garnish with coriander and drizzle with chilli oil to serve, if you like.

NOTE
*Many soy and Thai fish sauces contain gluten but gluten-free brands are available.

# THAI BEEF MASSAMAN CURRY
SERVES 4

Beef massaman curry is believed to have been brought to Thailand by Persian sea merchants and, judging from the spices used, it most likely was. You can see the Indian and Persian influences in the use of spices such as cinnamon, cardamom and cloves, which aren't seen in many Thai curries. You don't want to rush this one! The meat is cooked when it's cooked, so low and slow is the rule. Unlike many Thai curries, which include lots of different vegetables, massaman curries are made without vegetables in the sauce. That is unless you choose to add them, of course. Although massaman curries are normally served with rice, you might find you don't need it with those potatoes.

PREP TIME: 10 MINS
COOK TIME: 2 HOURS

700g (1lb 9oz) stewing beef
2 potatoes, peeled and cut into
  bite-size pieces
2 tbsp rapeseed (canola) oil
½ red onion, quartered
Handful of roasted peanuts
1 batch of massaman curry paste
  (see page 16)
400ml (1¾ cups) thick coconut
  milk
1 tbsp palm sugar
1 tsp tamarind paste (see page 17
  or shop-bought)
3 tbsp Thai fish sauce*
Salt, to taste
Thai holy basil, to garnish

Place the beef in a saucepan and pour 500ml (2 cups) of water over it. Bring to a simmer and cook for 1½–2 hours until the meat is really tender. You will probably need to add more water but only add just enough to cover. You want the stock to be really flavourful from the beef. When the meat is almost tender enough to eat, stir in the potatoes and cook until fork tender.

While the meat is cooking, you can start making the curry. In a wok or large frying pan, heat the oil over a medium–high heat. When it begins to shimmer, add the onion and peanuts. Fry for about 3 minutes, then add the curry paste. Stir well to combine with the oil and onions.

Now add the coconut milk, sugar and tamarind paste, followed by the beef, potatoes, about 250ml (1 cup) of the cooking liquid and the fish sauce. Simmer for about 10 minutes to thicken.

Taste and adjust the seasoning, adding salt to taste. Garnish with a few leaves of holy basil and serve.

NOTE
*Many Thai fish sauces contain gluten but there are gluten-free brands available.

# YELLOW CHICKEN CURRY
SERVES 4

Like massaman curry, Thai yellow curry definitely has Indian influences: the yellow colour comes from the turmeric in the curry paste as well as the curry powder which is also used. Many people liken this curry to an Indian restaurant-style chicken korma because it is yellow and made with coconut. It is normally a bit spicier than a chicken korma, but you can adjust the amount of chillies in your curry paste or use less paste if using a shop-bought one. Serve this with the rice of your choice.

With this recipe I wanted to introduce another way you can prepare your curries without adding oil. At many good restaurants they use a method of cooking called 'cracking the coconut milk'. By cooking a little coconut milk in your pan to start with, the natural coconut oil splits from the coconut milk. This is plenty of oil to fry with. Even if your coconut oil doesn't split, this method will still work. Use the best-quality coconut milk you can find. If this method doesn't appeal to you, just add 2 tablespoons of oil to the wok/pan and carry on with the recipe.

PREP TIME: 10 MINS
COOKING TIME: 20 MINS

10 small waxy new potatoes, quartered
600ml (2¾ cups) thick coconut milk
2 tbsp rapeseed (canola) oil
1 batch of yellow curry paste (see page 17 or shop-bought to taste)
1 tbsp palm sugar
1 tbsp tamarind paste (see page 17 or shop-bought)
600g (1lb 5oz) skinless chicken thigh fillets, cut into bite-size pieces
1 tsp curry powder (see page 22 or shop-bought)
1 carrot, cut into thin rounds
2 tbsp Thai fish sauce*
10 baby plum tomatoes, halved (optional)

TO GARNISH
4 tbsp fried garlic (see page 148)
Chopped chillies (optional)
Chopped coriander (cilantro) leaves (optional)

Bring a saucepan of water to a boil and cook the quartered potatoes until soft, about 10 minutes. Drain and set aside.

Meanwhile, heat a wok or large frying pan over a medium–high heat and add 200ml (¾ cup) of the coconut milk. Watch it as it comes to a simmer. The coconut milk should split and you should see the coconut oil. If it doesn't, that isn't a problem; the oil is still there.

Add the curry paste and fry for about 30 seconds to cook off the rawness. Stir in the palm sugar and tamarind paste and then add the chicken. Fry for a couple of minutes, stirring continuously until the chicken is about 80% cooked through. Add the curry powder, carrot and the remaining coconut milk and simmer to thicken for about 5 minutes. Stir in the fish sauce, tasting and adjusting the flavours as necessary.

Stir in the cooked potatoes and tomatoes (if using) and serve hot, garnished with fried garlic and chopped chillies and coriander if you like.

NOTE

*Many Thai fish sauces contain gluten but there are gluten-free brands available.

# BEEF PANANG CURRY
SERVES 4

Panang curries are similar to red curries and can be on the spicy side. The main differences are that Panang curries include peanuts and are often thicker and sweeter than red curries, which is why no stock is added to this recipe. However, there is no reason why you couldn't make this curry just like the red curry on page 70 so that it is thinner and more soupy. If making this recipe as it's written, the thick sauce is delicious served over hot jasmine rice. Although authentic Panang curries are not cooked with vegetables, I have added baby sweetcorn, courgettes (zucchini) and mushrooms to mine, so leave them out if you want a more traditional flavour and presentation.

PREP TIME: 10 MINS
COOKING TIME: 20 MINS

2 tbsp rapeseed (canola) oil
600g (1lb 5oz) beef rib-eye, cut
   thinly against the grain
1 batch of Panang curry paste
   (see page 16 or shop-bought
   to taste)
1–2 tbsp palm sugar
600ml (2½ cups) thick coconut
   milk
About 225g (8oz) vegetables,
   such as chopped baby
   sweetcorn, courgette
   (zucchini), mushrooms
3 lime leaves, stalks removed
   and leaves finely julienned
2 tbsp Thai fish sauce* (more or
   less to taste)

Get that meat cooking first so that it becomes nice and tender. Heat the oil in a wok or large frying pan. When visibly hot, add the meat and fry for a couple of minutes to brown it. Add the curry paste and sugar, starting with just one tablespoon of the sugar. You can always add more for a sweeter flavour.

Add the coconut milk and simmer for about 5 minutes to thicken. Stir in your vegetables of choice and simmer for another few minutes until cooked through but still fresh and not at all mushy. Stir in the lime leaves and fish sauce. Taste the sauce, adding more sugar for sweetness or more fish sauce for a saltier flavour.

NOTE
*Many Thai fish sauces contain gluten but there are gluten-free brands available.

# DUCK JUNGLE CURRY
SERVES 4

Jungle curry has its origins in Chiang Mai in the north of Thailand. Traditionally, the ingredients used in jungle curry were those that could be found in the jungle. Game meat was at one time the meat of choice, but you are much more likely to see this on restaurant and takeaway menus with chicken, duck or pork. Unlike so many Thai curries, coconut milk isn't used. The broth should be spicy, thin and clear and full of meat and vegetables. This is great served with sticky rice, as pictured.

PREP TIME: 15 MINS
COOKING TIME: 15–20 MINS

4 duck breasts
2 tbsp rapeseed (canola), peanut or coconut oil
6 tbsp Thai red curry paste (see page 14 or shop-bought to taste)
500ml (2 cups) Thai chicken stock (see page 18 or shop-bought) or water
10 green (string) beans, cut into 2.5cm (1in) pieces
1 x 227g (8oz) tin (can) bamboo shoots, drained and cut into matchsticks
5 baby sweetcorn, cut into small pieces
3 tbsp fresh green peppercorns
2–3 tbsp Thai fish sauce*
6 lime leaves, stalks removed and leaves thinly sliced
Juice of ½ lime
1 tsp palm sugar (optional)
Coriander (cilantro) leaves, to garnish
Thai sweet basil leaves, to garnish

Heat a frying pan over a medium–high heat. When hot, place the duck breasts skin-side down and fry for about 5 minutes. Flip the breasts over and cook for another 2 minutes. The duck should still be nice and pink in the centre. Slice into thin bite-size or slightly larger than bite-size pieces and set aside.

Heat the oil in a large pan or wok over a medium–high heat. When visibly hot, stir in the curry paste and fry for about 30 seconds until really fragrant. Stir in the stock or water and bring to a rolling simmer. Add the sliced duck and let it cook in the stock for about 5 minutes or until cooked through.

Stir in the veggies and green peppercorns and simmer until cooked to your liking. I usually only cook mine for about 3 minutes as they will continue cooking in the hot curry sauce. Add the fish sauce, sliced lime leaves and lime juice. Taste the sauce and adjust, adding more fish sauce for a saltier flavour, sugar if you prefer it sweeter and more lime juice for more sourness. This is a spicy curry, so you could add a little more red curry paste or chilli powder too.

Once you have the flavour you are looking for, garnish with coriander and Thai sweet basil leaves.

NOTE

*Many Thai fish sauces contain gluten but there are gluten-free brands available.

# STIR FRIES

Who doesn't love a good Thai stir fry? These quick
and easy recipes are perfect when you need dinner in
a hurry, or as part of a multi-course Thai feast.

It goes without saying that it is essential that you use
the freshest ingredients you can get your hands on for
these stir-fry recipes.

# STIR-FRIED BEEF IN OYSTER SAUCE
SERVES 4

On Thai menus this is often called 'pad nam mun hoy', which means fried with oyster sauce. There are many versions of Thai oyster sauce curries, but this beef version is right up there when it comes to popularity. Stir-fried beef in oyster sauce usually also comes served with mushrooms and my favourite variety for this recipe are straw mushrooms, but you could use any type you can find – wild mushrooms work really well. Serve with a hot bowl of jasmine rice.

PREP TIME: 10 MINS, PLUS
MARINATING TIME
COOKING TIME: 20 MINS

350g (12oz) sirloin steak
2 tbsp light soy sauce*
2 tbsp rapeseed (canola) oil or
　sesame oil
4 garlic cloves, roughly chopped
Large handful (about 100g) of
　whole straw mushrooms
1 medium onion, thinly sliced
3–4 tbsp oyster sauce*
4 tbsp stock or water
$\frac{1}{2}$ tsp ground white pepper
1 tbsp cornflour (cornstarch),
　mixed with $1\frac{1}{2}$ tbsp water
4 spring onions (scallions), cut
　into 5cm (2in) pieces
1 red spur chilli, cut into thin
　rings

Slice the sirloin against the grain into thin 6mm (¼in) strips. Place in a bowl and add 1 tablespoon of the light soy sauce and 1 tablespoon of the oil. Mix well and leave to marinate for 10 minutes. For a more intense flavour, you could let the meat marinate for longer.

Heat the remaining oil in a wok over a medium–high heat. When the oil begins to shimmer, stir in the chopped garlic and fry for a couple of minutes until fragrant but not browned. Now add the marinated beef strips and stir-fry until browned, stirring continuously. This should only take a couple of minutes. Add the mushrooms and sliced onion and stir it all up to combine.

Pour in the oyster sauce, remaining soy sauce, stock or water and white pepper. Again, stir this quickly and then add the cornflour (cornstarch) and water paste. Bring to a simmer – the paste will cause the sauce to thicken and give it a shiny appearance. Don't forget to taste it and adjust the flavours to taste.

To finish, add the chopped spring onions (scallions) and chilli slices and stir a bit so that they are coated lightly in the sauce.

NOTE
*Many soy and oyster sauces contain gluten but gluten-free brands are available.

# THAI HOLY BASIL AND CHILLI CHICKEN STIR FRY
SERVES 4

**Although there is no rule about how to cut your chicken for this popular Thai stir fry, I like to cut the meat quite small, slightly smaller than bite-size. This is a delicious and easy recipe that can be whipped up in minutes. Serve it with white, steamed jasmine rice.**

PREP TIME: 10 MINS
COOKING TIME: 10 MINS

8 garlic cloves, smashed
5 red spur chillies, cut into
   thin rings
2 tbsp rapeseed (canola) oil
2 shallots, thinly sliced
600g (1lb 5oz) skinless chicken
   thigh fillets, cut into small
   pieces
1 tbsp light soy sauce★
1 tsp palm sugar, finely chopped
   (more or less to taste)
1 tbsp oyster sauce★
1½ tsp dark soy sauce★
Large handful of Thai holy basil
   leaves, finely or roughly
   chopped

Place the garlic and chillies in a pestle and mortar and pound until chunky and small but not smooth (this can also be done with a knife or food processor). Set aside.

Heat the oil over a high heat in a large wok or frying pan. When hot, add the shallots and fry for a couple of minutes until fragrant and softened. Stir in the garlic and chilli mixture and fry for about 30 seconds, being careful not to burn your garlic.

Now stir in the chicken pieces and fry for about 4–5 minutes until cooked through. Be sure to stir continuously so that the aromatic ingredients don't burn. With the chicken cooked through and nicely coated with the aromatic mixture, stir in the light soy sauce, sugar, oyster sauce and dark soy sauce. Taste it and add more chillies, sugar or light soy sauce to taste.

Turn off the heat and then add the basil (it tastes much fresher if it is simply stirred into the chicken at the end of cooking). That's it! Enjoy.

NOTE
★Many soy and oyster sauces contain gluten but gluten-free brands are available.

# CHICKEN WITH CASHEWS
## SERVES 4

This is a hugely popular dish at Thai restaurants and takeaways, and my family love it. It is important to cut the chicken pieces so that they are about the same size as the cashews (although this is more for presentation as large chunks also work fine). You can mix the sauce and fry the cashews, chillies and chicken a day or so in advance, making this a dish you can cook up very quickly after work with little mess. The first time I tried making this recipe, I burnt the cashews and chillies. Don't make the same mistake or you'll have to start all over again. They don't take long to colour in the oil and cashews aren't cheap, so keep an eye on them. Although there's nothing stopping you from doing so, the dried and fried chillies are not meant to be eaten. I like to serve this curry with jasmine rice.

PREP TIME: 20 MINS
COOKING TIME: 10 MINS

250ml (1 cup) rapeseed (canola) oil, plus an extra 3 tbsp
20–30 cashews
20 dried red bird's eye chillies
450g (1lb) skinless chicken thigh fillets, cut into small cashew-size pieces
3 tbsp cornflour (cornstarch)
6 garlic cloves, roughly chopped
1 large onion, thinly sliced
3 red spur chillies, thinly sliced
2 green bird's eye chillies, cut into thin rings
4 spring onions (scallions), sliced

FOR THE SAUCE

2 tbsp light soy sauce
1 tbsp dark soy sauce
1 tbsp oyster sauce
1 tsp Thai seasoning sauce (optional)
70ml (¼ cup) water or chicken stock (see page 18)
1 tsp palm sugar, grated and finely chopped

Whisk all of the sauce ingredients together and taste it. Add more sugar if you like a sweeter flavour and then set aside.

Heat 250ml (1 cup) of rapeseed (canola) oil in a wok or saucepan until shimmering hot. Add one cashew. It should sizzle on contact but not brown too quickly. If that cashew looks like it is happy in the oil, add the rest and cook for about a minute until light golden brown in colour. Transfer to a paper towel to soak up any excess oil. Do the same with the chillies, checking the oil temperature first. You want them to still be a nice deep red colour. If the oil is too hot, they will quickly burn and turn brown.

Dust the chicken pieces with the cornflour (cornstarch) and add it in small batches to the hot oil. Fry for 3–5 minutes until golden brown and crispy. Transfer to a paper towel to soak up the excess oil.

Now heat a wok or large frying pan over a medium heat. Add 3 tablespoons of oil to the wok and stir in the garlic, onion, spur chillies and green bird's eye chillies. Fry until the garlic is turning soft and a very light brown colour but be very careful not to burn it. Stir in the sauce mixture and simmer for about 30–60 seconds to thicken and then add the chicken, cashews and dried and fried chillies, stirring well to combine.

Continue cooking for a minute or two until the sauce is sticking to the meat and cashews and then taste it, adjusting the seasoning if necessary. Serve immediately sprinkled with the chopped spring onions (scallions) to garnish.

# SWEET AND SOUR PRAWN STIR FRY
## SERVES 4

So here we have one of my favourite stir fries: pad priew wan. 'Pad' means stir-fried, 'priew' means sweet and 'wan' means – you guessed it – sour. Like most of the recipes in this cookbook this can be made with many different main ingredients. Here I chose prawns (shrimp) so it's a pad priew wan goong, but what you make it with is up to you. This is a classic stir fry and it is really important to ensure all the ingredients are cooked to perfection at the same time. If you are new to stir-frying and want to ensure your prawns aren't overcooked or your veggies aren't too crisp or mushy, you could cook the prawns or other main ingredient and vegetables separately. This is a good idea if cooking something like beef or pork, but prawns and vegetables are usually finished cooking at about the same time. This stir fry is great hot served over jasmine rice.

PREP TIME: 15 MINS
COOKING TIME: 10 MINS

2 tbsp rapeseed (canola) oil
5 garlic cloves, roughly chopped
600g (1lb 5oz) small prawns
 (shrimp), peeled and deveined
100g (3½oz) diced tinned
 (canned) pineapple
1 onion, thinly sliced
1 cucumber, deseeded and diced
4 asparagus spears, cut into
 2.5cm (1in) pieces
2 medium tomatoes, quartered
3 spring onions (scallions) cut
 into 2.5cm (1in) pieces

FOR THE SAUCE
3 tbsp rice wine vinegar
2 tbsp oyster sauce*
2 tbsp pineapple juice
2 tbsp sriracha sauce (see page
 145 or shop-bought)
1 tbsp light soy sauce*
½ tbsp Thai seasoning sauce (or
 more soy sauce)*
1 tbsp grated palm sugar or
 honey

Start by whisking all of the sauce ingredients together. Taste it to ensure you have the right balance of sweet, spicy, sour and salty. Set aside.

Heat the oil in a large wok over a medium–high heat and toss in the garlic. Fry for 30–60 seconds until fragrant and only just beginning to turn a light brown. Add the prawns (shrimp) and stir-fry for a minute, stirring and moving your wok around continuously to coat the prawns with the garlic oil. When the prawns are turning light pink but aren't completely cooked through, stir in the pineapple, onion, cucumber and asparagus and fry for another couple of minutes until the prawns are cooked through and the vegetables are cooked but still slightly on the crunchy side.

Pour in the prepared sauce and stir well. Taste and adjust the seasoning and remove from the heat. Stir in the quartered tomatoes and coat them with the sauce and then garnish with the chopped spring onions (scallions).

NOTE
*Many soy, oyster and Thai seasoning sauces contain gluten but gluten-free brands are available.

# STIR-FRIED VEGETABLES
SERVES 4

If you like vegetable stir fries, go ahead and adapt this recipe using any vegetables of your choice. The most important thing is that you use the freshest, most in-season vegetables you can find. This simple stir fry is most often called pad pak ruam on menus. 'Pad' means stir-fried, 'pak' means vegetables and 'ruam' means mixed, and stir-fried mixed vegetables is exactly what you get here, with a tasty sauce cooked into them! This is great served with jasmine or sticky rice.

PREP TIME: 15 MINS
COOKING TIME: 10 MINS

2 tbsp sesame oil
6 garlic cloves, roughly chopped
2 green bird's eye chillies, cut
 into thin rings
150g (5½oz) young broccoli,
 roughly chopped
150g (5½oz) carrot, sliced into
 thin coins
150g (5½oz) baby sweetcorn,
 roughly chopped
150g (5½oz) mangetout
150g (5½oz) red (bell) pepper,
 thinly sliced
150g (5½oz) bean sprouts
150g (5½oz) straw mushrooms
 (or use any mushrooms)
10 baby plum tomatoes, halved

FOR THE SAUCE
2 tbsp light soy sauce*
1 tsp dark soy sauce*
3 tbsp oyster sauce*
2 tsp grated palm sugar or
 white sugar

Start by preparing the sauce. Whisk all of the sauce ingredients together along with 3 tablespoons of water in a bowl and set aside.

Heat the sesame oil in a large wok or pan over a medium–high heat. When hot, add the garlic and fry for about 30–60 seconds until fragrant and lightly browned. Be careful not to burn the garlic. Add the chillies, broccoli, carrot rounds and baby sweetcorn and fry for a couple of minutes, stirring regularly. Now add the mangetout, red (bell) pepper, bean sprouts and mushrooms and fry for another couple of minutes. Don't overcook the vegetables! They should be cooked through but not mushy.

To finish, stir in the prepared sauce and bring to a simmer. Stir the plum tomatoes into the sauce, then serve.

NOTE
*Many soy and oyster sauces contain gluten but there are gluten-free brands available.

# NOODLES

In this section you will find the most popular noodle
dishes served at Thai restaurants. There are a few tricks
I have learned over the years and I will share them with
you in the following recipes.

If you are just wanting to make a delicious Thai noodle
dish, you could use shop-bought dry noodles. If, on the
other hand, you want to take it all up a notch, try my
homemade rice noodle recipe on page 20.

# THAI DRUNKEN NOODLES
SERVES 4–6

You might wonder why this popular noodle dish is called Thai drunken noodles; I did too before I looked it up. The Thai name for this noodle dish is pad kee mau, which means 'fried drunkard'. It's believed that it was originally made when a man returned from the pub quite drunk and whipped this one up quickly with things he had in to feed his hunger. Another possible explanation is that it is great food for curing a bad hangover. Whatever the reason, this delicious restaurant noodle dish is one you can easily make at home.

PREP TIME: 15 MINS
COOKING TIME: 15 MINS

3 tbsp rapeseed (canola) oil
1 shallot, thinly sliced
12 garlic cloves, roughly chopped
2–3 green bird's eye chillies, thinly sliced
225g (8oz) diced chicken breast or thigh
5 spring onions (scallions), cut into 5cm (2in) pieces
200g (7oz) wide Thai dried rice noodles, soaked in lukewarm water for 30 minutes
Large handful of Thai sweet basil

FOR THE SAUCE
4 tbsp oyster sauce★
2 tbsp light soy sauce★
1½ tbsp dark soy sauce★
1 tbsp sugar

Prepare the sauce by mixing together all of the sauce ingredients in a bowl. Taste and adjust the flavours as you see fit, then set aside.

Heat a wok over a high heat and add the oil. When it begins to shimmer, add the sliced shallot and fry for about 2 minutes. Add the chopped garlic and chillies and fry for a further couple of minutes, stirring regularly. Now add the chicken and stir-fry for about 2 minutes until it is about 50% cooked through.

Pour in the sauce ingredients, the spring onions (scallions) and noodles. Don't worry about drying them off (just pick them out of the water), as any water that drips off them will help cook them. Submerge the noodles in the sauce and stir continuously. They will cook quickly but test them before serving. They really need to be covered in the sauce to cook until soft. There isn't a lot of sauce, so keep pressing them down until cooked.

Stir in some of the basil then serve immediately, garnished with the remaining basil.

NOTE
★Many soy and oyster sauces contain gluten but gluten-free brands are available.

# PAD THAI
SERVES 4

Probably the most famous of Thai noodle dishes, pad thai wasn't served until 1939. The Thais had been consuming rice noodles for centuries, but at that time Chinese wheat noodles were very popular in Thailand. Seeking to promote Thai nationalism, the then prime minister, Plaek Phibunsongkhram, not only supported changing the name of the country from Siam to Thailand, he also sought to promote cooking with rice noodles as a way of eliminating Chinese influence and cooking more with rice, which grows in abundance in the country. Pad thai is now served at pretty much every Thai restaurant and takeaway. This is my version of the dish.

PREP TIME: 20 MINS, PLUS
SOAKING TIME
COOKING TIME: 15 MINS

2 tbsp rapeseed (canola) oil
1 tsp dried shrimp
6 garlic cloves, roughly chopped
100g (½ cup) firm tofu, sliced
2 skinless chicken thigh fillets,
    cut into small pieces
2 eggs
6 jumbo prawns (shrimp),
    peeled and deveined
2 tsp salted turnip (optional)
200g (7oz) dried rice noodles
    soaked in bath-hot water for
    30 minutes or 400g (14oz)
    fresh noodles
5 spring onions (scallions), cut
    into 5cm (2in) pieces
150g (1½ cups) bean sprouts,
    plus extra to garnish
50g (¼ cup) dry-roasted
    unsalted peanuts, crushed
1 tsp roasted chilli flakes (see
    page 22)
Lime quarters, to serve

FOR THE SAUCE
5 tbsp Thai fish sauce*
2 tbsp sugar
70ml (¼ cup) tamarind paste
    (see page 17 or shop-bought)
1 tbsp fresh lime juice
1½ tbsp white distilled vinegar
1 tbsp sriracha sauce (see page
    145 or shop-bought)

Start by mixing the sauce ingredients in a bowl, adjusting to taste as necessary. Set aside.

Heat the oil in a wok over a high heat. When it begins to shimmer, add the dried shrimp and garlic and sauté for about 30 seconds. Add the tofu and chicken and brown in the oil for about a minute.

Push all of these ingredients to the side of the wok and crack the eggs into the empty side. Allow them to cook for about a minute and then stir the par-cooked egg into the other ingredients.

Add the prawns (shrimp) and let them cook with the other ingredients until about half cooked through. This should only take about a minute or two. Then add the sauce.

Stir in the salted turnip (if using) and the soaked or fresh rice noodles until the noodles are nicely coated in the sauce mixture. Fold in the spring onions (scallions) and bean sprouts – the hot noodles will cook the sprouts and onions but you are only really steaming them. Stir in half of the crushed peanuts and continue cooking until the noodles look wet but there isn't a lot of sauce left. You don't want the noodles dripping with sauce, they should just be moist from having cooked in the sauce.

Transfer to four heated plates and garnish with the remaining peanuts, the roasted chilli flakes and remaining bean sprouts. Serve with lime wedges.

NOTE

*Many Thai fish sauces contain gluten but there are gluten-free brands available.

# PAD SI EEW (FRIED NOODLES IN SOY SAUCE)
SERVES 2–4

Pad si eew is famous for the way the noodles are stir-fried over a high heat until they are beginning to brown. This gives them a delicious smoky flavour that simply has to be tried. It's also known for the amount of soy sauce used. Pad si eew means 'fried in soy sauce', after all.

You can used dried fat rice noodles for this recipe but traditionally it is made with homemade or shop-bought fresh rice noodles. If using fresh noodles, it is crucial that you prepare them correctly or the results could be disastrous. Be sure to take some time to completely separate the noodles before adding them to the wok. If your noodles are sticking together, place them in the microwave for about 30 seconds. It is easier to separate the noodles warm than when they are cold.

PREP TIME: 15 MINS
COOKING TIME: 15 MINS

6 tbsp rapeseed (canola) oil
5 garlic cloves, peeled and roughly chopped
200g (7oz) skinless chicken thigh or breast, cut into 2.5cm (1in) pieces
100g (3½oz) Chinese broccoli, stalks thinly sliced
450g (1lb) fresh rice noodles (see page 20 for homemade) or 300g (10½oz) dried wide rice noodles, soaked just before cooking as per packet instructions
2 large eggs
Roasted chilli flakes (see page 22), to serve
Pickled chillies (see page 147), to serve
1 tsp ground white pepper

FOR THE SAUCE
2 tbsp dark soy sauce*
3 tsp light soy sauce*
2 tsp white distilled vinegar (optional)
1 tsp oyster sauce*
2 tsp palm sugar or white caster sugar

Combine all of the sauce ingredients along with 2 tablespoons of water and set aside.

Heat the oil in a large non-stick wok or frying pan over a medium–high heat. Add the chopped garlic – no need to wait until the oil is hot – and fry for about 2–3 minutes until fragrant and lightly browned. Add the chicken and fry for a couple of minutes until it is about 80% cooked through. Then add the chopped broccoli and stir to combine.

Reduce the heat to low and add half of the noodles along with half of the sauce. Move the noodles around delicately to mix with the sauce. Don't stir them vigorously or they may fall apart. Add the remaining noodles and sauce and again move them around in the pan or toss them if you can. Sometimes I use my hands for this. The noodles will clump together a little. That is fine – you just want to avoid them falling apart too much. If they do, it's a cosmetic rather than a taste issue.

Lightly move the contents of your pan to one side of the wok/pan and crack open the eggs in the other side. Turn the heat back up to medium–high and scramble them. Then carefully fold the noodles, chicken and broccoli over the eggs. Give the wok/pan a couple of tosses and allow the underside of the noodles to char lightly in the pan. Using a spatula, or tossing or using your hands, try to turn the noodles over to char the other side. You will know your pad si eew is ready when the sauce is quite dry and some of the noodles have been seared crisp. They won't all get crispy!

Serve on plates topped with roasted chilli flakes and pickled chillies and sprinkled with a little white pepper.

NOTE

*Many soy and oyster sauces contain gluten but there are gluten-free brands available.

# RAD NA (PORK AND NOODLES WITH GRAVY)
SERVES 4

Rad na should be made with wide rice noodles, preferably homemade, though any flat rice noodles will work. It is best to cook your noodles over a medium to high heat to give them a bit of a char and smoky flavour. You can do this in advance, as they do at many Thai restaurants. 'Rad' means to pour in Thai and 'na' means top. That's what you will be doing here – pouring a delicious thick gravy all over the top of a nice pile of smoky seared noodles and pork. I recommend using a non-stick wok or pan for this one.

PREP TIME: 15 MINS
COOKING TIME: 15 MINS

250g (9oz) pork shoulder, sliced into small, bite-size thin slivers against the grain
450g (1lb) fresh rice noodles (see page 20 for homemade) or 225g (8oz) dried wide rice noodles, soaked just before cooking as packet instructions
2 tsp dark soy sauce*
2–3 tbsp rapeseed (canola) oil
200g (7oz) Chinese broccoli or other Asian greens, roughly chopped
Pickled chillies (see page 147), to garnish
Fried shallots (see page 148), to garnish

FOR THE MARINADE
2 tbsp tapioca starch
1 tbsp light soy sauce*
1 tbsp oyster sauce*
¼ tsp ground white pepper
1 egg white
1 tsp sesame oil
1 tsp Chinese cooking wine or dry sherry (optional)

FOR THE SAUCE
2 tbsp sesame oil
5 garlic cloves, finely chopped
2 tbsp yellow soy bean paste or Yeo brand gluten-free hot soy bean paste
500ml (2 cups) unsalted pork or chicken stock (see page 18)
2 tsp soy sauce*
1 tbsp palm sugar
2 tbsp tapioca starch

Start by making the marinade. Whisk all of the marinade ingredients in a bowl, adjusting to taste as necessary. Add the pork and let it sit while you prepare the rest of the dish, or leave it overnight to marinate.

If using homemade or shop-bought fresh noodles, separate them and place them loosely in a bowl. If they are difficult to separate, heat them in the microwave for 30 seconds. Pour the dark soy sauce over the rehydrated or fresh noodles, then mix it in with your hands.

Heat a non-stick wok or large frying pan over medium–high heat. Add about 1 tablespoon of the rapeseed (canola) oil and when it begins to shimmer add half of the noodles. Fry for about 20 seconds without stirring, then toss the noodles over in the wok/pan or turn them carefully with a spatula. If using fresh noodles, some clumping will occur. That's OK; you are trying to sear them so they turn crispy in areas. When they are turning crispy, pour them onto a warm serving plate and repeat the process with more oil and the remaining noodles.

Now for the sauce. Working swiftly, wipe your wok clean with a paper towel and add the sesame oil. Stir in the garlic and bean paste and fry for about a minute until the garlic is turning a light brown. Add the stock, soy sauce and sugar and bring to a boil. Meanwhile, whisk the tapioca starch with 2 tablespoons of water in a glass and set aside. When your sauce reaches boiling point, add the pork slowly and cook it through, stirring often at first so that it doesn't stick together. It is important that you don't add the pork too quickly to the boiling sauce so it maintains its heat. The sauce must be boiling when the pork is added or the protective marinade coating will fall off into the sauce rather than cooking onto the pork. After about 1 minute of simmering, add the broccoli and cook for a couple of minutes until tender.

To finish, stir in the tapioca starch paste a little at a time until the sauce thickens and glistens to your liking. You may not need it all; you just want a thick and smooth gravy. Taste and adjust the seasoning if necessary. Pour this delicious, thick gravy over the seared noodles. Garnish with pickled chillies and fried shallots.

NOTE
*Gluten-free brands are available for soy and oyster sauces.

You are more likely to find khao soi served at Thai restaurants and takeaways with small, bite-size pieces of boneless and skinless chicken breast or thigh. Here, however, I show you a more traditional way of doing it with chicken on the bone, which adds a nice flavour to the sauce. If you would prefer chicken off the bone, that's fine too, but you should add chicken stock to the sauce instead of water for optimum flavour. Khao soi means 'cut rice' because originally the noodle soup was made with cut rice noodles. Though that is still a popular option, nowadays you are much more likely to see khao soi made with boiled and fried egg noodles on top – optional but a real treat.

PREP TIME: 10 MINS
COOKING TIME: 30 MINS

FOR THE NOODLES
225g (8oz) dried Chinese flat
   egg noodles
Oil, for shallow-frying

FOR THE SOUP
2 tbsp rapeseed (canola) oil
1 batch of yellow curry paste
   (see page 17 or use 3–6 tbsp
   shop-bought)
800ml (3¾ cups) thick
   coconut milk
1 generous tbsp good-quality
   curry powder (see page 22 or
   shop-bought)
8 bone-in chicken thighs, halved
1–2 tsp grated palm sugar
1 tbsp Thai fish sauce
1–2 tbsp light soy sauce

TO GARNISH
Pickled chillies (see page 147)
Fried shallots (see page 148)
3 tbsp finely chopped coriander
   (cilantro) leaves
Roasted chilli flakes (see page
   22), to garnish

Bring about 3 litres (3 quarts) of water to a boil in a large saucepan. Add the dried egg noodles and cook for about 5 minutes until soft but still a bit al dente. Drain and rinse with cold water if not using within 30 minutes to prevent the noodles from sticking together. Take out about a quarter of the noodles and dry them on paper towels.

In a large saucepan or wok, bring 5cm (2in) rapeseed (canola) oil to shimmering point over a medium–high heat. When hot, fry the noodles you patted dry with paper towels in batches. Place a small amount in the oil and flatten them with a spatula. Fry for about 45 seconds and then flip them over. Fry for another 45 seconds and flip over again. Continue until the noodles are a light, golden brown and then transfer to paper towels to soak up the excess oil. Repeat with the remaining noodles you set aside.

To make the soup, heat 2 tablespoons of rapeseed oil in a large saucepan or wok. When hot, add the yellow curry paste and fry for about 30 seconds, then add half the coconut milk and the curry powder. Stir well to combine.

Add the chicken thighs, skin-side down, and simmer until the coconut milk has almost evaporated but the sauce is still moist. Pour in the remaining coconut milk, the palm sugar and 400ml (1¾ cups) of water and bring to a simmer. Cook the chicken for at least 20 minutes or for a little longer if that is more convenient.

Just before serving add the fish sauce and soy sauce to taste. At this stage, you could also add more sugar if you prefer a sweeter curry and/ or more curry paste if needed, but remember: if it's a spicy curry you're after, this is served garnished with spicy roasted chilli flakes!

When you are ready to serve, divide the boiled noodles equally between six bowls. Then divide the chicken between the bowls and cover each with the soupy sauce. Garnish with pickled chillies, fried shallots, coriander (cilantro) leaves and roasted chilli flakes, and then top each with a good piece of fried noodles.

# SINGAPORE NOODLES
SERVES 4

**This dish was probably first served by Chinese immigrants at Chinese restaurants in the US. It became so popular that Thai restaurateurs quickly included it on their menus too. Singapore noodles are mildly spiced, so this is great for those who don't like spice. For those who do, you can add red chilli flakes.**

PREP TIME: 15 MINS
COOKING TIME: 15 MINS

200g (7oz) dried rice vermicelli
    noodles
1 tbsp Shaoxing rice wine or
    dry sherry
1 tbsp light soy sauce*
1½ tsp cornflour (cornstarch)
150g (5½oz) prawns (shrimp),
    peeled and deveined
4 tbsp vegetable oil
2 eggs, beaten
200g (7oz) thinly sliced grilled
    char sui pork (see page 127,
    or shop-bought)
4 garlic cloves, finely chopped
1 tbsp finely chopped galangal
2 spring onions (scallions),
    finely chopped
1 onion, halved and thinly sliced
½ red (bell) pepper, sliced to the
    same size as the onion
½ green (bell) pepper, sliced to
    the same size as the onion
50g (2oz) sugar snap peas,
    trimmed and sliced diagonally
    into 3 pieces
100g (3½oz) bean sprouts
1½ tbsp mild curry powder (see
    page 22 or shop-bought)

## FOR THE SAUCE
250ml (1 cup) chicken stock
2 tbsp Thai fish sauce*
1 tbsp oyster sauce*
1 tsp palm sugar

## TO GARNISH
2 spring onions (scallions),
    sliced into 2.5cm (1in) pieces
2 red spur chillies, thinly sliced
Roasted red chilli flakes (see
    page 22), to taste (optional)

Whisk all of the sauce ingredients together, then taste and adjust the seasoning if needed. Set aside.

Cover the rice vermicelli with boiling water in a large bowl. Move the noodles around in the bowl so that they don't stick together. Leave for 2 minutes, then drain and cover with cold water until needed.

In another bowl, whisk together the Shaoxing rice wine or sherry, soy sauce and cornflour (cornstarch). Add the prawns (shrimp) and stir to combine, then set aside to marinate.

Now heat a wok over a medium heat and stir in 1 tablespoon of the oil. When hot, add the eggs and cook, without moving them, for about 15 seconds, then use a spatula to move them around and break up the egg into small pieces. Transfer the cooked egg to a bowl.

Wipe your wok clean with paper towel and add another tablespoon of oil. Add the prawns and cook for a couple of minutes until almost cooked through and then add the sliced char sui pork. Now add the garlic, galangal and finely chopped spring onions (scallions) and fry for another 30 seconds, moving everything around in the wok. Stir in the sliced onion and (bell) peppers and fry for another minute. Add the sugar snap peas and bean sprouts and stir it all well to combine. Pour this mixture into a bowl and wipe your wok clean with paper towel.

Add the remaining oil to the wok and stir in the soaked noodles and curry powder. Fry for about a minute while stirring continuously to ensure the curry powder coats the noodles. Pour everything back into the wok, including the sauce, and again stir well to combine.

To serve, garnish with the sliced spring onions and spur chillies and a sprinkle of roasted chilli flakes, if liked.

NOTE
*Many soy, oyster and Thai fish sauces contain gluten but there are gluten-free brands available.

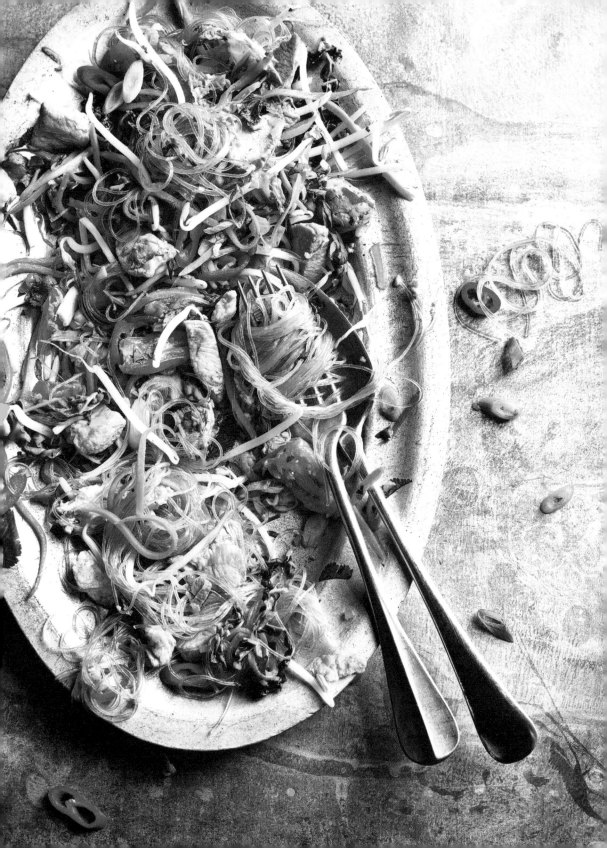

# STIR-FRIED GLASS NOODLES WITH CHICKEN
SERVES 4

Glass noodles (or cellophane noodles) are made from starch, such as mung bean starch or potato starch. They look a lot like rice vermicelli when dry but after cooking they are transparent and look more starchy. This is a classic way of stir-frying them. Here I've used chicken thighs, but pork, beef and tofu also work well. As with all noodle and stir-fry dishes, it's best to use a large wok for this one.

PREP TIME: 15 MINS
COOKING TIME: 15 MINS

125g (1 cup) diced chicken
1 tbsp light soy sauce*
150g (5½oz) glass noodle
    vermicelli
3 tbsp rapeseed (canola) oil
2 large eggs, beaten
4 garlic cloves, chopped
4 shallots, thinly sliced
2 red bird's eye chillies, thinly
    sliced into rings
1 medium carrot, grated
100g (3½oz) savoy cabbage,
    shredded
8 baby plum tomatoes, halved
200g (7oz) bean sprouts

FOR THE SAUCE
3 tbsp water or Thai chicken
    stock (see page 18)
1 tbsp Thai fish sauce*
1 tbsp light soy sauce*
2 tbsp oyster sauce*
¼ tsp white pepper
1 tsp palm sugar, grated and
    finely chopped

TO GARNISH
3 spring onions (scallions),
    sliced
1 red spur chilli, cut into rings
4 tbsp finely chopped coriander
    (cilantro)

Put the cubed chicken into a bowl, stir in the soy sauce and set aside. Soak the glass noodles in water for 10 minutes to soften and then drain them. If you are not using the noodles immediately, stir in a small amount of oil to stop them from sticking. Be sure to toss the noodles every 5 minutes or so to separate them.

Meanwhile, combine the sauce ingredients in a bowl and whisk until the sugar is dissolved. Taste and adjust the flavours as necessary, then set aside.

Pour 1 tablespoon of the oil into a wok or large frying pan over a medium–high heat and add the beaten eggs. Fry for a couple of minutes, or until the egg is scrambled and cooked through and then transfer to a plate. Set aside.

Add the remaining oil to the wok and add the chopped garlic and fry for 30 seconds, then add the shallots and chillies. Fry until the shallots have softened, about 3 minutes, but watch the garlic to ensure it isn't burning. Stir in the chicken and continue cooking until the chicken is about 80% cooked through and then add the grated carrot and cabbage. Cook for a further minute or so before stirring in the tomatoes and soaked glass noodles. Pour the sauce over the glass noodles and add the cooked eggs. Stir quickly and fry the noodles evenly to bring everything together.

To finish, stir in the bean sprouts. Transfer equal portions to four serving plates and garnish each with the spring onions (scallions), spur chilli and coriander (cilantro).

NOTE
*Many soy, oyster and Thai fish sauces contain gluten but there are gluten-free brands available.

# SPECIALS

So many people go right for the classic favourites when ordering at a Thai restaurant or takeaway. This makes sense as those red, green, yellow, Panang, massaman and jungle curries are so delicious! In this section, I wanted to showcase the other Thai recipes that, though not as famous, are equally as amazing.

You'll find delicious stewed meats, steamed and fried fish and even a couple of variations on the classic red curry. You are in for a treat with these, so be sure to give them a go.

# PORK LARB
SERVES 4–6

Think of pork larb as a Thai version of a meaty Bolognese sauce. It is delicious served simply with jasmine rice or sticky rice. If you feel like a real treat, try it as a starter wrapped in egg baskets (see page 30). Pork larb is served both hot and at room temperature. It is often served as a salad with lots of crunchy vegetables and a nice spicy dressing. It's so good served that way – you can see what I mean by substituting some pork larb for the turkey larb in the salad on page 57.

PREP TIME: 10 MINS
COOKING TIME: 15 MINS

2 tbsp rapeseed (canola) oil
500g (1lb 2oz) lean minced (ground) pork
4 shallots, thinly sliced
1 tbsp roasted chilli flakes (see page 22)
1 tbsp soy sauce*
1 tbsp Thai fish sauce*
1 tbsp palm sugar or caster sugar
1½ tbsp roasted and ground rice (see page 22)
4 spring onions (scallions), roughly chopped
1–2 tbsp lime juice

Heat the oil in a large pan or wok over a medium–high heat. When hot, add the pork and fry for about 5 minutes until cooked through. Add the sliced shallots and roasted chilli flakes and stir well to combine. Now add the soy sauce, fish sauce, sugar and roasted and ground rice and stir again. Taste and adjust the flavours as necessary.

To finish, stir in the chopped spring onions (scallions) and top with lime juice to taste.

NOTE
*Many soy and Thai fish sauces contain gluten but gluten-free brands are available.

# PHUKET PORK BELLY STEW
SERVES 4–6

Pork belly is one of my all-time favourite cuts of meat. When cooked right, it is so tender and juicy. I've had this served to me in lots of different restaurants and, although I have had some that were really good, I've also experienced some that just didn't make the cut. It is so important that you simmer the pork belly until it is fall-apart tender, or it will be chewy and a bit of a let-down. The long simmering time also adds to the amazing flavour. So the meat is ready when it's ready. No rushing this one. It is great served alongside jasmine rice.

PREP TIME: 15 MINS
COOKING TIME: 2 HOURS
10 MINS

8 garlic cloves
10 coriander (cilantro) stalks
1 generous tbsp black
   peppercorns
2 tbsp rapeseed (canola) oil
1kg (2lb) pork belly, cut into
   bite-size chunks
5cm (2in) piece of cinnamon
   stick
2 star anise
2 tbsp palm sugar, finely
   chopped
3 tbsp light soy sauce*
2 tbsp dark soy sauce*
2 tbsp oyster sauce*
2 tbsp Chinese rice wine
6 tbsp finely chopped coriander
   (cilantro)

Put the garlic, coriander stalks and black peppercorns in a pestle and mortar and pound to a paste. Set aside.

Heat the oil in a saucepan over a medium–high heat. When it begins to shimmer, toss in the pork belly cubes and brown on all sides. This should take about 5 minutes but you might need to do this in batches. Transfer the browned meat to a plate and set aside.

Add the cinnamon stick and star anise to the remaining oil in the pan and let the spices infuse into the oil for about 30 seconds. Return the meat to the pan and add the sugar, soy sauces and the oyster sauce. Stir well until the sugar dissolves and then add the Chinese rice wine, the prepared paste and just enough water to cover the meat. Simmer for about 2 hours, or until the pork is fall-apart tender. You might need to top up with a little water from time to time.

When the pork is ready, taste and adjust the flavours as necessary, then stir in the chopped coriander and serve.

NOTE
*Many soy and oyster sauces contain gluten but there are gluten-free brands available.

# RED DUCK CURRY
SERVES 4

At Thai restaurants and takeaways, red duck curry is usually sweeter than other red curries. Some kind of fruit is usually added to the sauce such as pineapple or grapes, which gives this curry a flavour all its own; the sweeter flavour goes so well with duck meat. I have written this recipe using fried duck legs but I often use a whole roast duck, cut into about eight pieces. This is great served with stir-fried vegetables (see page 87) and sticky rice or jasmine rice.

PREP TIME: 10 MINS
COOK TIME: 1 HOUR 20 MINS

6 duck legs
1 batch of Thai red curry paste (see page 14 or shop-bought to taste)
2 tbsp palm sugar
400ml (1¾ cups) thick coconut milk
3 lime leaves, stalks removed and leaves finely julienned
2–3 tbsp Thai fish sauce*
225g (8oz) pineapple, cut into bite-size pieces
10 seedless green or purple grapes, halved
10 baby plum tomatoes, halved
2 red spur chillies, sliced, to garnish
Small bunch of Thai basil, roughly chopped, to garnish

Heat a wok or large, high-sided pan over a low heat and brown the duck legs, skin-side down, for about 15 minutes, turning from time to time. Once nicely browned, transfer to a plate.

Turn the heat up to medium–high and add the curry paste and fry in the duck oil for about a minute, then stir in the sugar to dissolve. Stir in the coconut milk and 500ml (2 cups) of water to deglaze the pan; bring to a simmer.

Add the browned duck legs and the lime leaves and simmer over a medium heat for about 1 hour, or until the duck meat is really tender. If you prefer a thicker sauce, turn the heat up to medium and reduce the sauce until you are happy with the consistency.

Stir in the fish sauce, pineapple chunks, grapes and tomatoes and cook for a further 2 minutes. Check for seasoning, adding more sugar for a sweeter flavour and/or more fish sauce for a saltier flavour. Pour into a serving dish and garnish with the sliced chillies and basil.

NOTE
*Many Thai fish sauces contain gluten but there are gluten-free brands available.

# RED PORK NUGGET CURRY
SERVES 4

I first tried this curry while in London during the photoshoot for my cookbook *The Curry Guy Bible*. I was already writing and researching for this cookbook and tried very hard to get the recipe from the restaurant. No way! It was the house specialty. I wasn't going to just give up and only get to eat this delicious curry when I happen to be in London, which isn't very often. Here is my interpretation of their simple but amazing dish. If you have a good chopper knife, cutting the ribs into nuggets is easy but a good butcher will do this for you and save you the time of doing it yourself. I serve this with jasmine rice but it's also great with sticky rice.

PREP TIME: 15 MINS
COOKING TIME: 1 HOUR

2 tbsp rapeseed (canola) oil
1 batch of Thai red curry paste (see page 14 or shop-bought to taste)
2 racks of meaty pork spare ribs, cut into small pieces
4 lime leaves, stalks removed and leaves finely julienned

Heat the oil in a large saucepan over a medium–high heat and add the curry paste. Fry the paste for about a minute and then add the pork rib nuggets. Brown them for a couple of minutes and then cover with water and add the lime leaves.

Simmer for 1 hour, or until the meat is fall-off-the-bone tender and the water has reduced into a thick sauce. You might need to add more water during cooking but the end result should be a thick sauce that sticks to the ribs.

Serve immediately.

# SPICY PORK AND GINGER RED CURRY
SERVES 4

This spicy, dry curry is called pad prik khing moo or something similar at restaurants and takeaways. What distinguishes this curry from others is that it is quite dry and usually stir-fried with green (string) beans. Although ginger is very popular in Asian cooking, Thais prefer to use galangal in most dishes. So khing dishes are different because they have a delicious flavour of ginger. To make this really authentic, make your own red curry paste (see page 14) with ginger instead of galangal. This dish is best served hot with jasmine rice.

PREP TIME: 15 MINS
COOKING TIME: 10 MINS

2 tbsp rapeseed (canola) oil
500g (1lb 2oz) pork shoulder, cut against the grain into thin, bite-size pieces
4 tbsp Thai red curry paste (see page 14 or shop-bought to taste)
225g (8oz) green (string) beans, cut into 2.5cm (1in) pieces
4cm (1½in) piece of ginger, peeled and julienned
6 lime leaves, stalks removed and leaves finely julienned
2 tbsp Thai seasoning sauce or light soy sauce (gluten-free brands are available)
2 tbsp Thai fish sauce (gluten-free brands are available)
1 tsp grated palm sugar or white sugar
1 red spur chilli, thinly sliced
Chopped coriander (cilantro) leaves, to garnish

Heat the oil in a wok or large frying pan. When shimmering hot, add the sliced pork and fry for a couple of minutes until almost cooked through. Stir in the curry paste and fry for another minute, being sure to coat the meat with the paste.

Add the beans, ginger and lime leaves and stir well. Pour in the seasoning/soy sauce, fish sauce and sugar. Continue cooking until the meat is cooked through and the sugar has dissolved.

Check for seasoning and then serve sprinkled with the sliced chilli and coriander (cilantro).

# CHOO CHEE SALMON
SERVES 4

Choo chee curries are very similar to red curries. Red curry paste is used to make the sauce and, just like red curries, coconut milk is a key ingredient. So what makes them different? The choo chee sauce is normally served over seafood, it is thicker than a normal red curry and also a bit sweeter. Choo chee curries are also not usually as spicy as a red curry. I have used salmon here but you could use any seafood. This sauce is just as good served over sea bass, scallops, prawns (shrimp) and it's often served over vegetables as a vegetarian option at many restaurants. In this recipe I have used a cooking method called 'cracking the coconut milk'. It is a traditional cooking style which can be used to cook coconut sauce curries without having to add oil.

PREP TIME: 10 MINS
COOKING TIME: 10 MINS

4 x 225g (8oz) salmon fillets
   with the skin on
2 tbsp rapeseed (canola) oil
2 tbsp finely chopped coriander
   (cilantro), to garnish
1 red spur chilli, thinly sliced,
   to garnish

FOR THE SAUCE
600ml (2½ cups) thick
   coconut milk
2 tbsp Thai red curry paste
   (see page 14 or shop-bought
   to taste)
5 lime leaves, stalks removed
   and leaves finely julienned
1 tbsp Thai fish sauce*
2 tsp grated palm sugar or honey

I like salmon cooked with a nice crispy skin. To do this, take a sharp knife and scrape it across the skin of each salmon fillet. As you do this, moisture will come out of the skin. Use a paper towel to dry this off your knife and continue scraping until the skin is paper dry.

Heat a non-stick frying pan over a medium–high heat and add the oil. When the oil is hot, place the salmon fillets in the pan and fry for about 3 minutes, pressing them down with your spatula so that the skin fries evenly. Flip the fillets over and cook the other side for a couple of minutes. I prefer my salmon pink in the centre but you could fry yours for longer if you prefer the salmon cooked through. Keep warm while you make the sauce.

Pour about a quarter of the coconut milk into a saucepan and bring to a simmer over a medium–high heat. As it simmers, the oil should separate from the milk. This is called cracking the coconut milk, a technique used a lot in Thai curries, but if yours doesn't separate don't worry too much.

Stir in the red curry paste and the remaining coconut milk and reduce down for a couple of minutes until it is much thicker. Stir in the lime leaves, the fish sauce and palm sugar or honey and continue simmering until the sugar dissolves into the sauce. Taste the sauce and add more sugar if you want it sweeter, more curry paste if you want it spicier and/or more fish sauce for a saltier flavour.

Place each salmon fillet, crispy-skin-side up, on four plates. Pour the sauce around the fish and also drizzle some over the top. Garnish with coriander and red chilli slices to serve.

NOTE
*Many Thai fish sauces contain gluten but there are gluten-free brands available.

# THAI-STYLE HAINANESE CHICKEN AND RICE
SERVES 4

This dish originates from China, where it is called Hainan chicken. The Thai version differs in its use of galangal instead of ginger and the Thai dipping sauces. This is a fun dish to serve, letting people mop up the sauces with chicken and rice and washing it down with hot chicken stock. Traditionally this is cooked in a clay pot, which adds to the flavour, but there's no need to run to the shop if you don't have one.

PREP TIME: 10 MINS
COOKING TIME: 1 HOUR

1.5kg (3lb 5oz) free-range chicken
7.5cm (3in) piece of galangal, sliced and lightly crushed
8 garlic cloves, smashed
20 black peppercorns
1 tsp salt
1 large onion, quartered
Large bunch of coriander (cilantro)
6 spring onions (scallions), roughly chopped
2 green or red bird's eye chillies, sliced in half
1 batch of jasmine rice (see page 138)
Chilli jam, sweet chilli sauce and/or nam jim jaew (see pages 142 and/or 144, or shop-bought), to serve

Put the chicken into a large saucepan and add the rest of the ingredients up to and including the chillies. Cover with cold water and bring to a boil over a high heat. Reduce the heat to low and simmer for 40 minutes, then cover the pan and allow to sit for a further 20 minutes, skimming off any foam that rises to the top.

Remove the chicken from the stock and place on a chopping board. Strain the broth (discarding the aromatics) and keep hot.

To serve, either carve the meat into thin slices or simply chop the whole chicken into about sixteen pieces. Pile the cooked rice on a serving platter, arrange the chicken on top and pour the hot chicken broth into four soup bowls.

Then dig in, dipping the chicken and rice into jam or sauce and the hot chicken broth.

# BAKED SALMON IN BANANA LEAF
SERVES 4-6

Cooking in a banana leaf is not only great for presentation, it also gives a delicious flavour to the fish. You can pick up fresh and frozen banana leaves at Asian shops, but if you can't get them, you can wrap the salmon in foil. This will lock in the juices of the fish, although you won't get the same flavour. This dish is delicious served with jasmine rice but I also love it with rice noodles and steamed broccoli.

PREP TIME: 10 MINS
COOKING TIME: 20 MINS

1 side of salmon (about 2kg/4½lb), skin removed if preferred
1 large banana leaf, washed (optional)
3 tbsp finely chopped coriander (cilantro), to garnish
Lime wedges, to serve

FOR THE SAUCE
5 tbsp runny honey
2 tbsp sriracha sauce (preferably Thai) (see page 145)
2.5cm (1in) piece of ginger, peeled and minced
5 garlic cloves, minced
1 tsp roasted chilli flakes (see page 22)
2 tbsp Thai fish sauce (gluten-free brands are available)
2 tbsp light soy sauce (gluten-free brands are available)
2 tbsp lime juice
4 lime leaves, stalks removed and leaves very finely chopped (optional)

Preheat the oven to 200°C (400°F/Gas 6). If needed, you can cut the salmon into two or more pieces so it fits more easily into a baking dish.

Place the sauce ingredients in a bowl and stir to combine. Taste and adjust the flavours as desired.

Place a large banana leaf inside in a baking dish and place the salmon on top. Pour the sauce over the salmon, then wrap tightly with the banana leaf. Place the dish in the oven and bake for 15–20 minutes, depending on the thickness of your salmon and your own personal preferences.

To serve, scatter with the coriander and serve with the lime wedges for squeezing over.

**Right:** Thai-style Hainanese chicken and rice with chilli jam (see page 142) and nam jim jaew sauce (see page 144)

# THAI STEAMED SEA BASS WITH LIME AND GARLIC SAUCE
SERVES 2–4

The first meal I ordered on my last trip to Bangkok was steamed fish with lime and garlic sauce. I'd tried it many different times in the US and UK but I wanted to see what it was like in Thailand. It wasn't just the sauce for the steamed fish that I was eager to try but the barramundi fish they used, as I had never come across it, either fresh or frozen, in the West. I found barramundi to be very similar to sea bass and equally as delicious. At Thai restaurants in the West you are much more likely to find this and other fish dishes served as fillets rather than whole fish. You can do that too if you prefer, but I like presenting the whole fish at the table.

PREP TIME: 10 MINS
COOKING TIME: 12 MINS

2 x 700g (1lb 9oz) sea bass,
  cleaned
20 lime leaves

FOR THE SAUCE
250ml (1 cup) Thai chicken stock
  (see page 18)
2 tbsp palm sugar
20 garlic cloves, finely chopped
6 red bird's eye chillies (more or
  less to taste), finely chopped
6 tbsp Thai fish sauce*
150ml (²⁄₃ cup) freshly squeezed
  lime juice
3 tbsp finely chopped coriander
  (cilantro)

Make three or four shallow slits on each side of the sea bass. Place the lime leaves in the cavity of the fish and place on a steaming tray. If you have a fish steamer, that is the best option, but any steamer that will hold the fish is fine.

Place the steamer over a high heat and steam the fish for about 12 minutes, or until cooked through.

While the fish is cooking, make the sauce. Heat the chicken stock in a saucepan over a medium–high heat and bring to a rolling simmer. Add the palm sugar and stir it into the stock until it dissolves. Turn off the heat and then add the chopped garlic. The sharp flavour of the garlic will mellow in the hot stock and become softer.

Stir in the chopped chillies followed by the fish sauce, lime juice and coriander (cilantro) and give it a good stir. Taste and adjust the flavours as necessary, then set aside.

Check the fish to see if it is cooked through; the flesh should easily come off the bone. If it is sticking, steam it for about another minute or so.

Place the cooked fish on a heated platter and spoon some of the garlic, chillies and coriander from the sauce over it. Then pour the remaining sauce over the fish. The sauce doesn't have to be piping hot as this is more of a salsa than a sauce but I do like mine to be warm. Serve immediately and enjoy.

NOTE
*Many Thai fish sauces contain gluten but there are gluten-free brands available.

# BUTTERFLY FRIED BREAM WITH LEMONGRASS SAUCE
## SERVES 2-4

Ask your fishmonger to prepare the bream for you and this Thai fried fish will be much easier to make. If you have a good sharp knife, you can do it yourself. Starting from the top of the fish, slice downwards from one side of the back bone, keeping your knife as close to the bones as you can so that you don't lose any meat. Slice all the way down but be careful not to slice through the skin on the bottom side. Repeat on the other side and then carefully remove the skeleton. Rubbing your hands over the butterflied fish, remove any pin bones that remain. Tweezers are good for doing this.

Fried fish is hugely popular done this way, not only in Thailand but at Thai restaurants here in the West. I love deep-fried fish and chips but this Thai recipe takes fried fish to a whole new and delicious level. The coriander (cilantro) and lime sauce with all that lemongrass just plain makes it!

PREP TIME: 20 MINS
COOKING TIME: 20 MINS

Rapeseed (canola) oil, for
   deep-frying
150g (1 generous cup) plain
   (all-purpose) flour
Salt and freshly ground black
   pepper, to taste
2 large sea bream, cleaned
   and butterflied
2 lemongrass stalks (white part
   only with outer layer
   removed), chopped, to garnish
2 red spur chillies, cut into thin
   rings, to garnish

FOR THE SAUCE
2 lemongrass stalks (white part
   only with outer layer
   removed), chopped
30g (1 cup) fresh coriander
   (cilantro)
70ml (¼ cup) freshly squeezed
   lime juice (approx. 2–3 limes)
2 tbsp Thai fish sauce
5 garlic cloves, smashed
1 generous tbsp finely chopped
   galangal (or use ginger)
3 green bird's eye chillies,
   roughly chopped
1 tbsp palm sugar or honey
2 tbsp coconut or rapeseed
   (canola) oil

To make the sauce, blend two chopped lemongrass stalks together with the coriander (cilantro), lime juice, 2 tablespoons of water, fish sauce, garlic, galangal, bird's eye chillies and sugar or honey until smooth. Taste and adjust the flavours as necessary.

Heat the coconut oil or rapeseed (canola) oil in a large frying pan. When hot, add the blended sauce and bring to a simmer. Keep warm.

Heat enough rapeseed oil to deep-fry the fish in a large wok or saucepan. You are aiming for a temperature of 180°C (350°F). Meanwhile, put the flour on a large plate and season with salt and pepper. Dust the butterflied fish with the seasoned flour, ensuring the whole fish is covered. Shake off the excess flour.

When the oil has reached frying temperature, slowly lower one of the fish into the oil and fry for about 8 minutes. Drain on a paper towel and keep warm while you repeat with the other fish.

Now add the chopped lemongrass stalks and sliced red chillies to the oil and fry for a few seconds until lightly browned. Transfer to a paper towel to soak up the excess oil.

Spoon some of the sauce on two heated plates and nestle the fried fish on top. Drizzle with more sauce and garnish with the fried sliced lemongrass and chillies.

# FRIED WHOLE SEA BASS WITH GARLIC AND CHILLI SAUCE
SERVES 1–2

This is an impressive and fun way to serve whole sea bass. Fish is served this way only at the best Thai restaurants, although serving whole fish is not to everyone's liking, so feel free to just fry fillets if you prefer. Getting the fish into an 'S' shape before frying helps it stay upright when served. I use a deep-fat fryer for this recipe, positioning the fish the way I want to present it in the basket before lowering it into the oil. You could do the same in a wok or pan by holding the fish in the 'S' shape and slowly lowering it into the oil.

PREP TIME: 10 MINS
COOKING TIME: 8 MINS

1 large whole sea bass, cleaned
Flour, for dusting (you can use fine rice flour if gluten-free)
Rapeseed (canola) oil, for deep-frying
3 spring onions (scallions), cut into 2.5cm (1in) pieces, to garnish
1 tbsp finely chopped coriander (cilantro), to garnish

FOR THE SAUCE
2 tbsp rapeseed (canola) oil
2 tbsp chopped garlic
2 red spur chillies, roughly chopped
2 red bird's eye chilies, roughly chopped
1 tbsp palm sugar or white caster sugar
1 tbsp tamarind paste (see page 17 or shop-bought)
2–3 tbsp Thai fish sauce*

Place the fish on a board and cut about six shallow slits at a 45-degree angle down each of the sides. Dust the fish lightly with the flour inside and out. You just want to lightly dust the fish, which will make it crispier when fried.

Heat your oil in a deep-fat fryer or wok to 180°C (350°F). When the oil is ready, completely submerge the fish by carefully lowering it into the oil in the swimming position, or 'S' shape. Fry for about 8 minutes until cooked through and crispy, then transfer to a paper towel to soak up the excess oil.

Now make the simple, quick sauce. Heat the 2 tablespoons of oil in a frying pan over a medium heat. Add the garlic and chillies and fry for about 3 minutes, being careful not to burn the garlic. Stir in the sugar, tamarind paste and fish sauce. Stir well to combine and bring to a simmer, then turn off the heat. Taste and adjust the sweetness with more sugar or the saltiness with more fish sauce.

Place the sea bass upright on a warm plate. Cover with the chilli and garlic sauce and garnish with chopped spring onions (scallions) and coriander (cilantro).

NOTE
*Many Thai fish sauces contain gluten but there are gluten-free brands available.

# FROM THE GRILL

Thai grilling and barbecuing is some of the best in the
world. Those flavours go so well with smoke! From the
world-famous weeping tiger steak served with nam jim
jaew sauce to Thai baby back ribs and gai yang, you will
find all the restaurant and takeaway favourites here.
If you like seafood, you've simply got to try the salt-
crusted fish. The meat is so succulent and tastes so
good dipped in seafood sauce.

So get those marinades prepared and go for it. Fire
up your grill and enjoy some insanely delicious Thai
barbecue. I should add here that, even though the curries
in this book are not cooked on the barbecue, there is no
reason you shouldn't. I love cooking curries outside too.

# PREPARING YOUR BARBECUE FOR DIRECT HEAT COOKING

Cooking over open flames is the simplest of the two methods used. When food is exposed to intense direct heat, it gets a wonderful, smoky char on the exterior, while the interior remains deliciously juicy.

When preparing the charcoal, it is a good idea to build a two-level fire. For ease, use a barbecue chimney starter to light the coals. When the coals are white-hot, pour the charcoal into the basin of the barbecue, then spread the charcoal so that two-thirds of the coals are stacked about twice as high as the remaining one-third. This way, you can easily move whatever it is you are cooking from the hot side of the grill to the cooler side if it begins to burn before it's cooked through.

I use a lot of charcoal (about two full shoe boxes) as it is important to achieve that intense heat. To check if the coals are ready, hold your hand about 5cm (2in) above the cooking grate. If your hand becomes uncomfortably hot in 2 seconds, you're ready to start cooking.

# PREPARING YOUR BARBECUE FOR INDIRECT HEAT COOKING

This method is used for roasting and you will need a barbecue that has a tight-fitting lid. Fill the barbecue on one side only with about two shoe-boxes full of charcoal, leaving the other half empty. Use a few firelighters to light the charcoal and let it burn until white-hot, then place the grill on top and whatever it is you are cooking over the side with no coals. Cover the barbecue and leave to cook. If you are barbecuing for a long period of time, you will need to throw a few handfuls of charcoal on the fire every 30 minutes or so.

# WEEPING TIGER STEAK
SERVES 4

This has to be one of my Thai restaurant favourites. I love a good steak, especially when flame-grilled. There are many explanations as to how this delicious steak dish got its name. Some say that it was originally made with brisket in northern Thailand. Before cooking, the meat was so tough that tigers couldn't eat it so they cried about it. Modern-day weeping tiger steak, sometimes called crying tiger, is made with deliciously tender marbled rib-eye steaks. It retained its name as the word 'weeping' refers to the juicy steaks dripping into the coals, simulating the tigers' tears. Another explanation is that the steaks are served with nam jim jaew sauce, which is so spicy it would make a tiger cry. By the way, this sliced steak is also delicious served at room temperature or as a salad. Try the dressing from my turkey larb salad (see page 57) with your favourite salad greens and enjoy it mixed with the steak slices and topped with a few tablespoons of toasted sesame seeds.

PREP TIME: 10 MINS, PLUS RESTING AND OPTIONAL MARINATING TIME
COOKING TIME: 10 MINS

4 x 225g (8oz) well-aged rib-eye steaks
Rapeseed (canola) oil, for brushing the grill
Nam jim jaew (see page 144 or shop-bought), to serve (optional)

FOR THE MARINADE
2 tbsp dark soy sauce*
1 tbsp light soy sauce*
1 tbsp Thai fish sauce*
2 tsp palm sugar
3 garlic cloves, minced
½ tsp freshly ground black pepper
1 tbsp rapeseed (canola) oil

Whisk together all of the marinade ingredients in a large bowl and add the steaks. Make sure that the steaks are completely coated with the marinade and allow to rest while you set up your barbecue. For best results you could let the steaks marinate overnight, but this isn't essential.

Set up your barbecue for direct heat cooking (see page 121). When your coals are white-hot and it is uncomfortable to hold your hand 5cm (2in) above the cooking grate, you're ready to cook. Lightly brush the cooking grate with oil and place the steaks over the coals. Cook to char for about 2 minutes and then flip the steaks over to char the other side. Continue turning until your steaks are cooked to your preferred doneness. If you have a meat thermometer, aim for 50°C (122°F) for rare, 60°C (140°F) for medium and 70°C (160°F) for well done. I prefer mine rare!

Transfer to a board to rest for 5 minutes and then slice into 6mm (¼in) slices against the grain. Serve with nam jim jaew, if you like.

NOTE
*Many soy and Thai fish sauces contain gluten but gluten-free brands are available.

# THAI-STYLE BABY BACK RIBS
SERVES 4–6

I think that pork ribs was the first meal I ever learned to make. This is party food, so I only make these for special occasions as they take a long time to cook. It's fun time though – sitting around in the garden, drinking beer and anxiously waiting for those succulent, tender ribs to hit the table. The key to cooking amazing ribs is to cook them low and slow. That, and of course, this recipe which will get you Thai restaurant-quality ribs every time. I normally use a wood pellet smoker for ribs. A normal barbecue works really well too, but you have to watch it more closely. You can also make these ribs in the oven. You will need foil for this recipe and a spray bottle is also useful.

PREP TIME: 15 MINS, PLUS
OPTIONAL MARINATING TIME
COOKING TIME: 4 HOURS

4 meaty racks of pork baby
  back ribs
4 tbsp rapeseed (canola) oil
70ml (¼ cup) rice wine vinegar
  or lime juice (whichever
  flavour you prefer)
Nam jim jaew (see page 144 or
  shop-bought), to serve
  (optional)

FOR THE DRY RUB
2 tbsp coarse sea salt
2 tbsp finely ground black
  pepper
2 tbsp garlic powder
1 tbsp roasted chilli flakes (see
  page 22) or chilli powder
4 tbsp palm sugar, finely grated
  and chopped (or use soft light
  brown sugar)

FOR THE BARBECUE SAUCE
6 garlic cloves
2 shallots, thinly sliced
2 tbsp finely chopped coriander
  (cilantro) stalks
1 tbsp palm sugar, grated
3 tbsp light soy sauce*
2 tbsp Thai fish sauce*
2 tbsp oyster sauce*
2 tsp sesame oil

Score the thin membrane on the bottom side of the ribs about 20 times. Many chefs will tell you to remove it, but I don't. It gets nice and crispy, so why waste it? Rub the pork racks all over with the oil. Mix the dry rub ingredients together and then rub this all over the ribs. If time permits, cover with cling film (plastic wrap) and marinate in the fridge for about 3 hours, but you can skip this step if you're in a rush.

When you are ready to cook, set up your barbecue for indirect heat cooking (see page 121), or set your wood pellet smoker to 135°C (275°F). This is the cooking temperature that you want to cook at for the whole cooking time of 4 hours. After the ribs have been cooking on this low heat for 1 hour, spray or brush them with vinegar or lime juice to keep the meat moist. Repeat again after 30 minutes.

Meanwhile, prepare the barbecue sauce. In a pestle and mortar, pound the garlic, shallots, coriander (cilantro) stalks and palm sugar to a fine paste. Add the remaining ingredients and stir well to combine. Adjust the flavours to taste as necessary, then set aside.

Once the ribs have been cooking for 2 hours, lay out four pieces of foil that are large enough to wrap each rack. Take the rib racks off the barbecue and place each on a piece of foil. Brush each liberally with about half the barbecue sauce. Wrap them tightly in the foil and place back on the barbecue to continue cooking for another hour. Wrapping them like this helps ensure they are really juicy and tender.

After 1 hour, unwrap the ribs and paint with the remaining barbecue sauce, and cook for another hour, unwrapped.

Your ribs will now be super juicy and fall-apart tender. Serve with nam jim jaew if desired.

NOTE
*Many soy, oyster and Thai fish sauces contain gluten but there are gluten-free brands available.

# PORK KNUCKLE
SERVES 4

Kao ka moo is a delicious Thai braised pork dish, popular at Thai restaurants, and is usually made with pork leg. It is so nice slowly brazed in the authentic way but here I have decided to mix it all up with this Thai/German-inspired schweinshaxe, or roasted ham hock. I lived in Germany for a few years while at uni and pork schweinshaxe was one of my favourite dishes. The meat is so tender and that crispy crackling is to die for. Serve this Thai-inspired pork knuckle and sauce with jasmine rice or rice noodles and a good dipping sauce, such as nam jim jaew (see page 144).

PREP TIME: 15 MINS
COOKING TIME: 3 HOURS
20 MINS

4 pork shanks, skin scored
Salt and freshly ground black pepper
2 tbsp rapeseed (canola oil)
2 medium onions, roughly chopped
1.5 litres (6 cups) water or unsalted pork or chicken stock
4 tbsp soy sauce*
4 tbsp oyster sauce*
2 tbsp dark soy sauce*
1 generous tbsp palm sugar or other sugar
10 coriander stalks, roughly chopped
8 garlic cloves, smashed
2 red spur chillies, roughly chopped
5cm (2in) piece of cinnamon stick
2 star anise
2 tsp Szechuan peppercorns
½ tsp black peppercorns, cracked
2 tbsp smashed and finely chopped galangal
2 shiitake mushrooms

Season the bottom of each shank with salt and pepper. Heat the oil in a large saucepan over a medium–high heat and fry the bottom of the shanks for about 4 minutes. Place the seared pork shanks into a large roasting tin that will fit comfortably on your barbecue. Fire up your barbecue with about one shoe box full of charcoal.

Using the oil and meat fat from frying the pork shanks, add the chopped onions to the pan and fry for about 3 minutes. Add the remaining ingredients to the pan and simmer until reduced by a third. Taste and adjust the flavours as necessary. Pour this sauce into the roasting tin with the pork shanks.

When the barbecue coals are white-hot, push them all to one side for indirect cooking (see page 121). Place the roasting tin on the grill over the half that has no charcoal, cover the barbecue with a lid and roast for 2 hours. The perfect roasting temperature to aim for is 120°C (250°F). You will need to top up the charcoal every 30 minutes to maintain that heat.

After 2 hours, remove the roasting tin from the barbecue. Strain the sauce through a fine sieve and keep warm. Put the meat back in the roasting tin and add a couple more shoe boxes of charcoal to the hot coals to bring your barbecue temperature up to 230°C (450°F). The charcoal still all needs to be on one side of your barbecue.

When that high heat is reached, place the pork shanks back on the barbecue, cover with the lid and cook for another 30 minutes over indirect heat. Cook for 30 minutes, or until the crackling is nice and crispy. The crackling will become crispier as it rests when removed from the barbecue.

Transfer the shanks to plates and drizzle the sauce over the top.

NOTE
*Many soy and oyster sauces contain gluten but there are gluten-free brands available.

# CHAR SUI PORK
## SERVES 6

This is actually a family recipe that I have been making for family and friends since my college years. Yes, it is Chinese not Thai, but it is one of the key ingredients needed to make the amazing Singapore noodles on page 99 – also not Thai. So we have two dishes that are not Thai, but they are both loved at so many Thai restaurants and takeaways that I felt I had to include them. This recipe makes a lot more than needed for the Singapore noodles recipe. You can freeze any leftovers for future use, although we rarely have any leftovers at my place by the time everyone stops snacking!

PREP TIME: 10 MINS, PLUS
MARINATING TIME
COOKING TIME: 45 MINS

1.5kg (3lb 5oz) pork shoulder

### FOR THE MARINADE
3 tbsp soft light brown sugar
2 tbsp dark soy sauce*
2 tbsp light soy sauce*
3 tbsp Chinese rice wine or
    dry sherry
3 tbsp honey
3 tbsp ketchup
1 tbsp Chinese five spice
2 tbsp rapeseed (canola) oil
½ tsp freshly ground black
    pepper
3 garlic cloves, finely minced
1 tsp red food colouring
    (optional)

Put all of the marinade ingredients up to and including the garlic into a saucepan. Place over a medium heat and bring to a simmer. Stir well until the sugar dissolves into the sauce and the sauce becomes nice and thick. This will only take about 2–3 minutes. Stir in the food colouring (if using). Allow to cool to room temperature.

Meanwhile, prepare the pork. Slice the pork shoulder with the grain into about three strips and then cut each piece against the grain through the centre. When the marinade has cooled, place the pork into a large glass or ceramic bowl and cover it with the marinade. Allow to marinate for 24–48 hours (the longer the better).

When you are ready to cook, set up your barbecue for indirect heat cooking (see page 121). You will need a couple of shoe boxes of charcoal as you want the barbecue to reach a cooking temperature of 180–200°C (350–400°F).

Once your barbecue is up to heat, take your pork and rub off the marinade (keep the marinade to use as a glaze). Place the pork in a roasting tin and place on the cool side of your barbecue. Cover the barbecue with the lid and allow to cook for 10 minutes and then quickly raise the lid and baste with the marinade. Cook for another 10 minutes and repeat. Cook for a final 10 minutes and brush with the glaze once more.

Serve hot or place in the fridge or freezer to use in stir fries and noodle dishes.

### NOTE
*Many soy sauces contain gluten but gluten-free brands are available.

# PORK NECK SKEWERS
SERVES 6

Pork neck or shoulder is a very popular cut in Thai cooking because of the meat-to-fat ratio. It's a very tasty cut. These skewers are great served with sriracha sauce (see page 145).

PREP TIME: 30 MINS, PLUS FREEZING
AND MARINATING TIME
COOKING TIME: 15 MINS

900g (2lb) pork neck or shoulder

FOR THE MARINADE
5 garlic cloves, finely chopped
2 tbsp finely chopped coriander (cilantro) stalks
2 tbsp finely chopped palm sugar or honey
1 tbsp Thai fish sauce★
1 tbsp soy sauce★
1½ tbsp oyster sauce★
1 tsp ground white pepper
200g (1 cup) unsweetened thick coconut milk

Cut the pork into 5cm (2in) wide strips, going with the grain. Place the pork in the freezer for 30–45 minutes. This will help make slicing easier. Meanwhile, put all of the marinade ingredients into a large bowl and whisk until smooth.

When the pork slices are really cold, place them on a board. Cut them it into 2cm (¾ in) pieces, this time going against the grain. Place in the marinade and set aside for at least 30 minutes. The meat will benefit from a longer time in the marinade, so let it marinate overnight if you can.

Prepare your barbecue for direct heat cooking (see page 121) with about a shoe box or two of charcoal. When the coals are white-hot and your hand is uncomfortably hot when held just above the grill for 2 seconds, you're ready to cook.

Skewer the meat so that the pieces are squeezed tightly together. Place on the grill, cook for about 5 minutes, then turn and cook for another 5 minutes. Check for doneness and cook a little longer if needed.

NOTE
★Gluten-free brands for these sauces are available.

# GRILLED PORK STEAKS
SERVES 6

Much quicker and simpler than the pork neck skewers, this recipe uses the same cut of meat but served as steaks. Pork neck or shoulder doesn't need a lot done to it to be amazingly delicious but it does have a lot of fat, so when cooked as steaks, it's essential to pound the meat with a meat mallet. I like to serve these with sauces such as nam jim jaew or chilli jam but you could just serve with lime wedges.

PREP TIME: 20 MINS, PLUS MARINATING TIME
COOKING TIME: 10 MINS

1kg (2lb 2oz) pork shoulder, cut into wide steaks about 1cm (½in) thick
Lime wedges, to serve
Chill jam or nam jim jaew (see page 142 or 144, or shop-bought), to serve (optional)

FOR THE MARINADE
3 tbsp grated palm sugar or white sugar
2 tbsp oyster sauce★
1 tbsp Thai fish sauce★
1 tbsp Thai seasoning sauce or light soy sauce★
1 tbsp rapeseed (canola) oil

Place the pork steaks on a board and pound each with a meat mallet until nice and thin. Turn them over and do the same again. You aren't trying to destroy them! You just need to tenderize them. Whisk the marinade ingredients together and rub it into the steaks. Allow to marinate for at least 30 minutes, or overnight if you have time.

When you are ready to cook, set up your barbecue for direct heat cooking (see page 121). When your coals are white-hot and you can't hold your hand 5cm (2in) above the grill for more than 2 seconds, you're ready to cook.

Place the pork steaks on the grill and cook for about 5 minutes each side until nicely charred and tender. Serve with lime wedges and your choice of Thai sauces if you wish. Amazing!

NOTE
★Gluten-free brands for these sauces are available.

**Right:** Pork neck skewers

# SALT-CRUST BREAM
## SERVES 2

When I learned to make salt-crust bream, there was no turning back! I love cooking fish this way. It is hugely popular at street-food stalls all over Thailand and, like many good things, it eventually made its way onto the menus in the West. The scales are left on the fish so that the meat doesn't become too salty. Caking the skin in all that salt keeps almost all the moisture in the flesh (the skin dries out and is not eaten). Simply peel the skin off and enjoy the juicy fish meat with some seafood dipping sauce (see page 144). You don't eat the aromatics but they give off an amazing aroma when served. I have tried this with larger, scaled fish and it was still very good.

PREP TIME: 10 MINS
COOKING TIME: 40 MINS

2 large whole sea bream (about
  1kg/2lb 2oz each), cleaned
  but not scaled
4 garlic cloves, smashed
1 thumb-sized piece of galangal,
  sliced into about 10 pieces
4 lemongrass stalks, lightly
  smashed
10 lime leaves (or use 1 sliced
  lime)
Approx. 425g (1½ cups) coarse
  sea salt
1 generous tbsp plain (all-
  purpose) flour
Seafood dipping sauce (see page
  144), to serve

Set up your barbecue for direct heat cooking (see page 121) while you prepare the fish. You only need to use one shoe box of charcoal as the fish needs to be cooked over a low heat.

Place the bream on a clean work surface and fill the cavities with the garlic, galangal pieces, lemongrass and lime leaves, dividing equally. Use lime leaves if you have them but sliced limes will work almost as well.

Pour the salt and flour into a bowl and mix it with just a tablespoon or two of water until it is fluffy and slightly moist to the touch. Start rubbing the salt all over the fish, pressing down slightly to help it stick. Flip the fish over and do the same on the other side.

When you are ready to cook, check your barbecue to make sure that your coals are not too hot. Grilling fish over hot direct heat would normally only take about 8–10 minutes; here you want to slow this down so that the fish cooks slowly. Lightly grease the grill and place the fish directly on it. Cook over the low heat for 15 minutes without turning, then, using a fish knife or metal spatula, carefully turn the fish over, taking care not to lose the salted skin on the grill. (Don't rush this or you will.) Cook the other side for a further 10 minutes, then carefully turn again. Keep turning every 5 minutes or so.

After 30–40 minutes, your bream should be cooked through and lightly browned from the heat and smoke.

To serve, place the fish on a warm platter. Peel the skin off the fish. Sometimes I use scissors or a sharp knife to help remove the skin. Cut into the meat and dip away!

# CHARGRILLED FISH
SERVES 4

Getting grilled fish right on the barbecue is a skill. Luckily, it isn't a difficult skill to learn. I used to grill fish in a barbecue fish basket but these really aren't needed here and you will get a much more attractive grilled fish if you don't use one. The trick is to get your grill good and hot and not to turn the fish too soon. Turn it too early and that lovely grilled fish skin will stick! I have used wild sea bass for this recipe, but any large fish, such as sea bream or snapper, will work well too. I always serve this with homemade Thai seafood dipping sauce (see page 144).

PREP TIME: 10 MINS, PLUS
MARINATING TIME
COOKING TIME: 10 MINS

2 x 1.5kg (3lb 5oz) wild sea bass, cleaned with fins removed and tail trimmed
2 generous tbsp Thai green curry paste (see page 14 or shop-bought)
1 tsp rapeseed (canola) oil, plus extra for brushing
6 lime leaves, stalks removed and leaves finely julienned
1 tbsp lemongrass, white part only, sliced as thinly as you can
2 red spur chillies, thinly sliced
2 tbsp finely chopped coriander (cilantro)

TO SERVE
Lime wedges
Pickled chillies (optional, see page 147)
Seafood dipping sauce (see page 144)

Place the sea bass on a board and score each fish 10–15 times on each side. Whisk the green curry paste with 1 teaspoon rapeseed (canola) oil and then rub this into the cavities and over the exterior of the fish. Cover and place in the fridge to marinate for 1 hour, or less if you are pressed for time.

Set up your barbecue for direct heat cooking (see page 121). When your coals are white-hot and your hand is uncomfortably hot when held 5cm (2in) above the grill, you're ready to get cooking.

Lightly brush the grill with oil. Standing at your barbecue so that the grill irons are running perpendicular to (away from) you, lay each fish on the grill with the cavity facing you. Cook for 5 minutes without moving the fish. Then carefully turn each fish over with a spatula. There should be no resistance. If the skin is still sticking to the grill, cook a little longer until it is no longer sticking.

Once flipped, you will have two beautiful fish with nice char marks on them. Cook the other side the same way, only removing the fish when they are cooked through and not sticking to the grill. Transfer each fish to warmed plates and scatter over the julienned lime leaves, sliced lemongrass, chillies and coriander. Serve with lime wedges and, for an extra special chilli hit, I recommend serving this with pickled chillies and, of course, seafood dipping sauce.

# GAI YANG (SLOWLY GRILLED THAI CHICKEN)
SERVES 4–6

The traditional way of cooking this butterflied chicken is quite a chore. Four bamboo skewers are tied on both sides of the chicken with a piece of wire to assist in turning the bird while cooking. I rarely bother with this and instead use a good, strong pair of tongs. I used to butterfly chicken by cutting out the backbone. In Thailand I noticed that it was done by slicing down the centre of the breasts, which is better as the chicken lies flatter on the grill. It is important to cook over a low flame so that the chicken gets a nice deep brown colour without being excessively charred. This is great served with nam jim jaew (see page 144).

PREP TIME: 20 MINS, PLUS
MARINATING TIME
COOKING TIME: 1 HOUR
20 MINS

1 x 1.5kg (3lb 5oz) whole chicken

FOR THE MARINADE
1½ tbsp black peppercorns
20 garlic cloves
1 lemongrass stalk
2 tbsp finely chopped coriander
  (cilantro) stalks
1 tbsp palm sugar
4 tbsp tamarind water (see
  page 17)
2 tbsp light soy sauce
2 tsp dark soy sauce
2 tsp Thai fish sauce

Place the black peppercorns in a pestle and mortar and pound to crack them. Add the garlic cloves and continue pounding until you have a thick paste. Throw in the lemongrass and coriander (cilantro) stalks and continue pounding so that all of the ingredients are coarsely ground with no really big bits. Stir in the remaining marinade ingredients and transfer to a large bowl or deep plate.

Place the chicken upright on a board on its legs so that it looks like it is sitting down. Using a sharp knife, slice downwards between the two breasts to butterfly it. Put the butterflied chicken into the marinade and rub the marinade all over it. I usually loosen the skin too and rub some of the marinade under the skin so that it is in direct contact with the meat, but this is optional. Set aside to marinate for at least 30 minutes while you set up your barbecue for direct heat cooking (see page 121). For best results allow the chicken to marinate overnight, but this isn't necessary.

When you are ready to cook and the coals are white-hot, spread them out a little so that the heat isn't too intense, as this is a slow cooking process.

Place the chicken on the grill, skin-side up first, and grill for about 20 minutes. Turn it over and cook for 10 minutes. Then flip over again and continue cooking until the chicken has been on the grill for about 1 hour 20 minutes, or until cooked through. Be sure to check your coals regularly so that you get a medium heat that is not too hot.

When the chicken is cooked, transfer to a board to rest for about 10 minutes and then cut into about eight pieces to serve.

# CHICKEN LEMONGRASS SKEWERS
SERVES 6

This delicious chicken dish uses lemongrass stalks for the skewers, although you could use wooden ones if you prefer. These skewers are great with sticky rice and nam jim jaew or sweet chilli sauce (see pages 141, 144 and 142).

PREP TIME: 15 MINS, PLUS MARINATING TIME
COOKING TIME: 15 MINS

3 lemongrass stalks (white parts only), finely chopped, plus extra stalks for the skewers
3 shallots, finely chopped
4 lime leaves, stalks removed and leaves finely chopped
2 red spur chillies, finely chopped
4 garlic cloves, crushed
1 tbsp finely chopped galangal
1 tbsp palm sugar or honey
1$\frac{1}{2}$ tbsp dark soy sauce (gluten-free brands available)
1$\frac{1}{2}$ tbsp oyster sauce (gluten-free brands available)
1 tbsp Thai fish sauce (gluten-free brands available)
900g (2lb) skinless chicken thigh fillets, thinly sliced

Place all of the ingredients except the chicken in a food processor or blender and blend to a paste. Tip into a bowl, add the chicken and turn to coat in the marinade. Set aside to marinate while you fire up your barbecue, which will take about 30 minutes. You could marinate the chicken overnight, which would be even better.

Set up your barbecue for direct heat grilling (see page 121). When the coals are white-hot and your hand is uncomfortably hot after holding it above the grill for 2 seconds, you're ready to cook.

If you are using wooden skewers, it is best to soak them in water for 30 minutes to stop them burning. (I often do this with lemongrass skewers too, but it's not strictly necessary.)

To use lemongrass stalks as skewers, use the woody green ends only (keep the white parts for cooking) – you'll need 6–8 skewers for this recipe.

Skewer the chicken on to the skewers or lemongrass stalks and grill for about 5 minutes per side, or until the chicken is cooked through.

# GRILLED PRAWNS
SERVES 4 OR MORE

Good fishmongers and Asian shops will have the prawns (shrimp) you're looking for to make this masterpiece of a meal. I tend to look for extra-large prawns, although you could, of course, use smaller prawns for this recipe or – if you've got a fat wallet – jumbo prawns. The thing I like most about this street-food recipe is its simplicity. Just grill the prawns and start dipping! One of the drawbacks of cooking prawns with the shell on is deveining them. With larger prawns this is easy, and you don't even need a knife. Look at the back of a prawn and bend it. You should see the vein through the shell. Take a toothpick and slide it under the vein at the second joint and pull up. You can then grab the vein and pull it out.

PREP TIME: 10 MINS
COOKING TIME: 10 MINS

20 large prawns (shrimp) with heads and shells on
Seafood dipping sauce (see page 144), to serve

Prepare your barbecue for direct heat grilling (see page 121). When your coals are white-hot and it is uncomfortable to hold your hand for two seconds above the grill, you're ready to cook.

Place all the prawns (shrimp) in a barbecue fish basket. If you don't have one, you could just put them right on the grill but you'll need to do a bit more turning. Put the fish basket with the prawns in it on the grill and cook for about 3 minutes, or until the prawns are turning pink and have blackened in some places. Turn the fish basket over and continue cooking until the prawns are an amazing red and black colour.

Pour these hot cooked prawns onto a serving plate. Give everyone some dipping sauce and get stuck in!

# RICE, SAUCES AND GARNISHES

Rice plays a big role in Thai meals. In fact, in Thailand it is so important that the translation for 'Have you eaten?' is 'Have you eaten rice?', even if rice isn't part of the meal!

Curries and barbecued dishes are usually served with either jasmine rice or sticky rice depending on what part of Thailand you are in (sticky rice with northern Thai dishes and jasmine rice with southern-style dishes). In the West, however, most people order whichever they prefer. Although plain jasmine and sticky rice are the most common, I have included a few other favourites too.

Sauces also play a big role in the perfect Thai meal. You will find the most popular sauces in the following pages, all of which are quick to make. Adding extras such as pickled chillies, fried garlic or fried shallots to a dish can also be so good – even if the recipe doesn't call for it.

# PLAIN JASMINE RICE
SERVES 4

The first time I cooked basmati rice, I treated it as I had been taught to cook jasmine rice. It was a complete failure. Although both of these popular aromatic rice varieties look very similar, the way you prepare them is completely different. Jasmine rice goes so well with Thai food. The grains are thicker and naturally softer than basmati and the cooked rice is also slightly sticky, making it perfect for moulding into shapes, as is so often done at restaurants. Also, unlike basmati and other rice varieties, it should never be soaked before cooking.

PREP TIME: 5 MINS
COOKING TIME: 30 MINS

370g (2 cups) jasmine rice

Put the rice into a bowl and cover with cold water. Swirl the water around a few times with your hand. The water will turn milky white. That's the starch on the rice and most of it should be rinsed off so that the cooked rice isn't too sticky. Pour this water away and repeat one or two times more until the water is almost clear. Drain and then tip the rice into a saucepan that has a tight-fitting lid. Add 750ml (3 cups) of cold water.

Cover with the lid and bring to a boil over a high heat. Once boiling, reduce the heat to low and simmer, covered, for about 15 minutes. Remove from the heat and allow to steam for an additional 10 minutes without lifting the lid.

Check the rice. If there is any water left in the pan, cover again until all the water has been absorbed. Stir lightly with a fork to loosen the grains and serve.

NOTE
Plain jasmine rice is normally served exactly as implied: plain, without any seasoning or butter.

# COCONUT RICE
SERVES 4

While travelling in Thailand I didn't see coconut rice served anywhere, except as part of a salad. I'm sure you could find it somewhere but it is much more of a Western Thai restaurant/takeaway thing – and people in the West do seem to love it. Like all Thai food, you need to adjust this dish to taste. I prefer mine a bit savoury with only the natural sweetness of the coconut, but you could add more sugar if you prefer a sweeter flavour.

PREP TIME: 5 MINS
COOKING TIME: 30 MINS

370g (2 cups) jasmine rice
175ml (¾ cup) coconut milk
1 tsp salt
1 tsp sugar (more or less to taste)

Put the rice into a bowl and cover with cold water. Swirl the water around a few times with your hand. The water will turn milky white. That's the starch on the rice and most of it should be rinsed off so that the cooked rice isn't too sticky. Pour this water out and repeat one or two times more until the water is almost clear. Drain and then tip the rice into a saucepan that has a tight-fitting lid. Add 175ml (¾ cup) of water along with the coconut milk, salt and sugar.

Cover with the lid and bring to a boil over a high heat. Once boiling, reduce the heat to low and simmer, covered, for about 15 minutes. Use your nose – there is fat in the coconut milk and it has a tendency to catch on the bottom of the pan. I like it but if you don't, be sure to remove from the heat if you believe it is sticking to the bottom. Remove from the heat and allow to steam for an additional 10 minutes without lifting the lid.

Check the rice. If there is any liquid in the pan, cover again until all the water has been absorbed. Stir lightly with a fork to loosen the grains and serve.

# GARLIC RICE
SERVES 4

This garlic rice is delicious with barbecued meats. Butter isn't used a lot in Thai cooking but I like it in this recipe. It may not be authentic, but butter is used at some pretty nice Thai restaurants, so why not? You need to watch your garlic as it fries; if it burns it will taste bitter. I like to cook mine until golden brown, a bit crispy yet soft on the inside.

PREP TIME: 5 MINS
COOKING TIME: 30 MINS

370g (2 cups) jasmine rice
3 tbsp unsalted butter
10 garlic cloves, roughly chopped
1/2 tsp salt, plus extra to taste
3 spring onions (scallions), cut into thin rings
3 tbsp finely chopped coriander (cilantro)

Put the rice in a bowl and cover with water. Swirl the water around a few times with your hand. The water will turn milky white. Pour this water out and repeat one or two times more until the water is almost clear. Drain and set aside.

Melt the butter in a saucepan over a medium heat, then add the garlic. Fry until it just starts to turn a light golden brown – about 5 minutes. For sweeter-tasting garlic, cook over a low heat for about 20 minutes. When light brown, transfer with a slotted spoon to a bowl and set aside.

Pour the rice into the pan and stir to coat it with the butter. Add the salt and 750ml (3 cups) of water. Cover and bring to a boil over a medium–high heat. Once boiling, reduce the heat to low and simmer, covered, for about 15 minutes. Remove from the heat and allow to steam for an additional 10 minutes without lifting the lid. Check the rice. If there is any water in the pan, cover again until all the water has been absorbed. Stir lightly with a fork to loosen the grains.

Add all but about 1 tablespoon of the garlic and stir it into the rice. Season with salt and garnish with the spring onions (scallions), coriander (cilantro) and the remaining garlic to serve.

# PINEAPPLE FRIED RICE
SERVES 4

Fried rice should always be made with cold cooked rice. If you add it freshly cooked and hot, it is likely to overcook and turn to mush. So not only is this recipe delicious, it is also a great way to use up leftover rice. This looks great served in a hollowed-out pineapple.

PREP TIME: 10 MINS
COOKING TIME: 15 MINS

1 fresh pineapple
3 tbsp rapeseed (canola) oil
4 garlic cloves, roughly chopped
1 tbsp shrimp paste
20 cashews
5 coriander (cilantro) stalks, finely chopped
2–3 red bird's eye chillies, finely chopped
12 small prawns (shrimp), peeled and deveined
1 egg
400g (2 1/2 cups) cold cooked jasmine rice
2 tbsp Thai fish sauce (gluten-free brands are available)
3 tbsp finely chopped coriander (cilantro) leaves

Slice the top off the pineapple and, standing it upright on a board, scoop out the flesh, discarding the tough core. Cut the flesh into bite-size pieces. Using a spoon, scoop out 3 tablespoons of the juice and set aside.

Heat the oil in a wok or large frying pan over a medium–high heat and add the garlic. Fry for about a minute, stirring continuously, taking care not to burn it. Stir in the shrimp paste, cashews, coriander (cilantro) stalks and chillies and fry for a further minute. Add the prawns (shrimp) and stir-fry until pink and just cooked through.

Push this mixture to one side of the wok/pan and crack the egg into the other half. Scramble it with your spatula as it cooks and stir it into the prawn mixture. Add the rice and fish sauce and stir well so each grain is coated with the oil and fry for a couple of minutes, lightly stirring as you do.

Stir in the pineapple chunks and pineapple juice and garnish with coriander to serve.

# STICKY RICE
SERVES 4–6

Thai sticky rice is a staple of northern Thailand. It is consumed all over Thailand, although never with coconut-milk-based curries or soups. That really doesn't matter in Western Thai restaurants and takeaways, where it is simply one of the rice options on the menu. Sticky rice can be enjoyed with whatever curry or soup you wish.

Special cooking vessels and steamers are used in Thailand to cook this famous and delicious rice, but you could use any steamer that will hold the rice. For a recipe this size, I use a round Chinese bamboo steamer, which you will find at most Asian grocers and online, but it is not necessary.

PREP TIME: 5 MINS, PLUS
SOAKING TIME
COOKING TIME: 15–20 MINS

675g (3 cups) Thai glutinous rice
(see note)

Pour the rice into a bowl and cover with water. Swirl the rice around in the water with your hand. The water will become milky white from the starch. Drain and repeat this process until the water runs almost clear.

Now cover the cleaned rice with about twice the volume of clean water and soak for 6 hours or overnight. It is important to cover with a lot of water as the rice will double in size as it soaks.

When ready to steam, place your steamer over a saucepan of boiling water and steam, covered, for 15 minutes. Check it – it should be sticky, fragrant and mouthwateringly delicious. You can cook it longer, as I do when I cook mango sticky rice (see page 150), but 15 minutes usually suffices when served as a side dish.

NOTE
It is important to use Thai glutinous rice but please don't mistake the word glutinous with glutenous. The word glutinous refers to the starch that is on the rice grains, rather than suggesting there is gluten in it (this would be glutenous). All rice is gluten-free.

# SWEET CHILLI SAUCE
MAKES 250ML (1 CUP)

You can of course buy Thai sweet chilli sauce at most supermarkets, but in my experience it just doesn't compare to homemade, as most shop-bought chilli sauces are lacking in substance. With this recipe you will produce a sweet chilli sauce that is loaded with chillies and garlic. You can adjust the heat level too. The mild large red spur chillies are there for colour and the red bird's eye chillies are there for heat. Use more bird's eye chillies if you want more heat or omit them and just use the milder chillies. This sauce is really sweet, which is why all the sugar is required.

PREP TIME: 10 MINS
COOKING TIME: 15 MINS

7 garlic cloves, roughly chopped
5 large red spur chillies, roughly chopped
4 red bird's eye chillies (more or less to taste), thinly sliced
100g (½ cup) sugar
4 tsp white malt vinegar
1 tbsp Thai fish sauce (gluten-free brands are available)
½ tsp tapioca flour or cornflour (cornstarch) (both are gluten-free)
Salt, to taste

Put the garlic and chillies into a food processor and blend until roughly chopped; alternatively you can do this with a knife.

Bring 150ml (⅔ cup) of water to a boil over a medium–high heat and add the sugar. Simmer until the sugar dissolves, then stir in 3 teaspoons of the vinegar, the chopped garlic and chillies and the fish sauce. Reduce the heat to low and simmer for an additional 5 minutes.

Whisk the tapioca flour or cornflour (cornstarch) with the remaining teaspoon of vinegar and then whisk this paste into the sauce. Taste it and add more fish sauce or salt if you prefer a saltier flavour.

Allow to cool and pour into a jar with a tight-fitting lid. This can be stored in the fridge for at least 2 weeks.

# CHILLI JAM
MAKES APPROX 400ML (1¾ CUPS)

Chilli jam, or nam prik pao, is a good one to have in your Thai recipe library. 'Nam prik' means chilli dip and 'pao' means roast or burn. That's exactly what you're getting here. Perfectly roasted, fresh ingredients with a delicious spicy bite.

PREP TIME: 15 MINS
COOK TIME: 5 MINS

2 banana shallots, peeled and roughly chopped
10 large garlic cloves, roughly chopped
10 dried red bird's eye chillies, cut into small pieces
10 red spur chillies, roughly chopped
2 tbsp dried shrimp
1 tsp shrimp paste
2 tbsp palm sugar or caster sugar
2 tbsp tamarind paste (see page 17 or shop-bought)
1 thumb-sized piece of galangal, finely chopped
3 tbsp Thai fish sauce (gluten-free brands are available)
125ml (½ cup) rapeseed (canola) oil

Heat a dry frying pan or wok over a medium–high heat and add the roughly chopped shallots and garlic. Move the garlic and shallots around in the pan continuously until they begin to smoke and char in places. Be careful not to burn the garlic; we are just toasting it. Transfer to a plate to cool.

Add the chillies to the pan and toast lightly until fragrant. This should only take about 40 seconds. Transfer to the plate with the garlic and shallots.

Put the garlic, shallots and chillies into a food processor along with all the remaining ingredients plus 2 tablespoons of water and blend for about a minute until you have a thick paste. Transfer to a wok or frying pan and fry until the colour has darkened by about two shades and the oil is separating from the paste. Taste it and add more sugar for extra sweetness, more fish sauce if you like it saltier or more tamarind for sourness. Whisk the separated oil into the jam.

Blend again if needed and store in a sterilized jar (see page 147) in the fridge. This jam will keep for a good 2 weeks.

**Clockwise from top left:** Sriracha sauce (page 145); chilli jam (above); sweet chilli sauce (left); pickled chillies (page 147); spicy shallot pickle (page 147)

# NAM JIM JAEW
## (THAI MEAT DIPPING SAUCE)
MAKES 250ML (1 CUP)

Nam jim jaew is the perfect accompaniment for all meats. It is pictured on page 122 next to the weeping tiger steak. Be sure to adjust these ingredients to taste. If you want to make things easier on yourself, you can buy nam jim jaew at Asian shops and online, but this one is so simple – I definitely think it's worth the effort of making it yourself.

PREP TIME: 10 MINS

3 tbsp Thai fish sauce★
4 tbsp tamarind water (see page 17)
1 tbsp palm sugar or white sugar
1 tbsp roasted chilli flakes (see page 22)
1 tbsp roasted and ground rice (see page 22)
1½ tbsp lime juice
2 shallots, finely chopped
1 red spur chilli, finely chopped (optional)
2 tbsp finely chopped coriander (cilantro) stalks
2 spring onions (scallions), cut into thin rings

This one couldn't be easier! Simply put all of the ingredients into a bowl and whisk to combine. It is important to taste as you go so that you get the perfect blend of sweet, sour and spicy.

NOTES
You can make this a few days in advance and keep in an airtight container in the fridge if that is more convenient.

★Many Thai fish sauces contain gluten but gluten-free brands are available.

# THAI SEAFOOD DIPPING SAUCE
MAKES APPROX. 250ML (1 CUP)

There's a reason this is called seafood dipping sauce... it's so good with seafood – all seafood! Make a batch of this and serve it as a dip for any simple fish meal. It really packs a punch. It is pictured on page 34.

PREP TIME: 10 MINS

6 green bird's eye chillies, roughly chopped
4–6 red bird's eye chillies, roughly chopped
8 garlic cloves, smashed
5 tbsp chopped coriander (cilantro) leaves and stems
1 tbsp oyster sauce★
3 tbsp Thai fish sauce★
125ml (½ cup) lime juice
2 tbsp sugar

Put the chillies, garlic and coriander in a pestle and mortar or food processor and pound or blend to a chunky paste.

Tip into a bowl, add the remaining ingredients and taste, adding more sugar for sweetness and/or a little more fish sauce if a saltier flavour is desired. This dipping sauce is excellent with all fish and seafood. Try it with the salt-crust bream on page 130 and you won't be disappointed.

NOTE
★Many oyster and Thai fish sauces contain gluten but gluten-free brands are available.

# SRIRACHA SAUCE
MAKES 250ML (1 CUP)

Making sriracha sauce is easy and it tastes great too. Once made, you can adjust the heat for future batches to your preference. Bird's eye chillies are very spicy while spur chillies are much milder, although they do have a kick to them. I tend to do a 50/50 mix of the two. Most commercial brands use a lot of flavour enhancers and stabilizers, giving them an artificial flavour and a longer shelf life. This recipe will give you the real thing. It is pictured on page 143.

PREP TIME: 10 MINS, PLUS FERMENTING TIME
COOKING TIME: 15 MINS

225g (8oz) red bird's eye chillies
225g (8oz) red spur chillies
10 garlic cloves
1½ tbsp palm sugar
1 tbsp salt
70ml (¼ cup) distilled white vinegar

Put the chillies, garlic cloves, sugar and salt in a food processor and blend to a coarse paste. Scoop it all into a glass bowl and cover with cling film (plastic wrap). Leave to ferment for 2 days at room temperature. You will know that it is fermenting nicely when small bubbles appear on top. Uncover and stir well and then cover again and leave for 3 more days, stirring every 24 hours or so.

On the fifth day, pour the mixture into a blender with 70ml (¼ cup) of water and the vinegar and blend until very smooth. Pass the smooth paste through a fine sieve into a saucepan, pushing down on the solids with the back of a spoon to try and get as much as possible into the pan.

Cook over a medium–high heat until it begins to simmer and then reduce the heat to medium and cook for about 15 minutes to thicken. Pour into sterilized glass jars (see note on page 147) to cool and then cover with the lids. This sauce will keep in the fridge for up to 4 weeks without losing much flavour.

# CUCUMBER AND CHILLI RELISH
SERVES 4

This cucumber and chilli relish, pictured on page 34, is one of the most recognized Thai relishes and is one you need in your recipe library. It's not only delicious but also very colourful. Be sure to taste it as you prepare it to get the perfect flavour balance for you.

PREP TIME: 5 MINS, PLUS CHILLING TIME
COOKING TIME: 30 MINS

80ml (⅓ cup) white distilled vinegar
2 tbsp sugar
1 tsp salt
½ English cucumber, diced
3 small shallots, thinly sliced
2 red spur chillies, thinly sliced
2 tbsp finely chopped coriander (cilantro)

Place a saucepan over a low–medium heat and add the vinegar, sugar and salt. Bring to a simmer and cook until the sugar and salt have dissolved.

Add the cucumber, shallots and red chillies to the warm liquid. Allow to cool for about 20 minutes, then stir in the coriander (cilantro). Place in the fridge and allow to chill for at least 30 minutes or longer.

NOTE
You can make this a few days in advance and keep in an airtight container in the fridge if that is more convenient.

# CHILLI OIL
## MAKES ABOUT 750ML (3 CUPS)

This is a popular way of making chilli oil that is used a lot in Thai cooking, although you'll see from the ingredients that the finished oil needn't be limited to Thai cooking – spice up your next pizza with the oil and some of the goop at the bottom, for example. This oil is delicious served in the tom kha gai soup on page 62 or on top of a Thai red curry (see page 70). Although chilli oil is available from most Asian shops, nothing beats homemade.

PREP TIME: 15 MINS
COOKING TIME: 10 MINS

200g (7oz) dried red bird's eye chillies
10 fresh red bird's eye chillies
4 banana shallots, peeled
12 garlic cloves
600ml (2½ cups) rapeseed (canola) oil

Starting with the dried chillies, blend them in a small food processor into small chilli flakes. Set aside. Do the same with the fresh chillies, shallots and garlic cloves, blending them separately until finely chopped but not a paste. (All of this could of course be done with a knife but it takes longer.)

Heat the oil in a small saucepan over a medium–high heat. When hot, add the shallots and fry for about a minute until soft. Then add the garlic and fry for a further 30 seconds or so before adding the fresh chopped chillies. Continue to fry until the onion takes on a light golden brown colour and then stir in the dried chillies. This whole process should take no more than about 7 minutes.

Remove from the heat and allow to cool. Then pour the chilli oil into a sterilized glass container (see note on page 147) and keep in the fridge to use whenever you want a nice spicy oil.

# BASIL OIL
## MAKES 250ML (1 CUP)

Thai sweet basil oil tastes great and has many uses. I rarely strain the oil but it is done at some fancy restaurants. For me, I just like to blend it and use it. This adds a nice green colour to green curry (see page 69) and can also be used as a garnish for meat dishes. Alternatively, drizzle it over a salad such as the green papaya salad on page 54 or the turkey larb salad on page 57.

PREP TIME: 5 MINS
COOKING TIME: 5 MINS

60g (3 packed cups) Thai basil leaves (or use any basil)
250ml (1 cup) rapeseed (canola) oil

Bring a saucepan of water to a boil and add the basil leaves. Simmer the basil for a couple of minutes, or until the leaves are so soft that they tear really easily. Strain and place the basil in a bowl of iced water to cool.

Put the basil leaves in a blender and add the oil. Blend until smooth and green. You can either run the oil through a fine sieve and/or cheesecloth for a clear green oil or leave it as is. If straining, leave the oil for about an hour before doing so. This will give you a greener oil.

Pour the basil oil into a sterilized glass container (see note on page 147) and keep in the fridge to add to dishes whenever you desire a nice green colour. It is best used within a few days.

# PICKLED CHILLIES
MAKES 300ML (1¼ CUPS)

There's nothing fancy about this recipe. It's often used as a colourful garnish and is really good to have on hand. It is pictured on page 143. Although you really should let the chillies pickle in the vinegar for a few days, I often use them after about an hour.

PREP TIME: 3 MINS

250ml (1 cup) white distilled vinegar
10 red spur chillies, cut into 5mm (¼in) slices

Place the sliced chillies in the vinegar and pickle for at least 1 hour or overnight. These will keep for a long time in a sterilized glass jar with a lid.

NOTE
To sterilize jars, preheat the oven to 110°C (225°F/ Gas ¼). If your jars have rubber sealing rings on the lid, remove them and boil in water for 5 minutes. Wash the jars thoroughly in hot, soapy water and rinse well, then place on a baking tray in the preheated oven for about 15 minutes until dry. Carefully remove them from the oven and fill them while still hot.

# SPICY SHALLOT PICKLE
MAKES 250ML (1 CUP)

This easy pickle, pictured on page 143, can be whipped up in minutes. The flavours get better if you let it sit covered in the fridge for a few days, but it will be perfect if you simply make it and serve straight away. I love this pickle with barbecued meats or used as a garnish for stir fries.

PREP TIME: 10 MINS

4 banana shallots, thinly sliced
3 garlic cloves, thinly sliced
3 red bird's eye chillies, thinly sliced
3 tbsp lime juice
3 tbsp rice wine vinegar
1 tsp sugar
¾ tsp salt

Place all of the ingredient in a mixing bowl and stir together. Adjust the salt and sugar to taste. You can also add more chillies or lime juice. Leave for about 10–20 minutes and serve.

# FRIED SHALLOTS
MAKES APPROX. 250ML (1 CUP)

**Fried shallots are a popular garnish in Thai cuisine. This simple recipe will give you perfectly fried shallots every time.**

PREP TIME: 2 MINS
COOKING TIME: 10 MINS

3 tbsp rapeseed (canola) oil
6 shallots, thinly sliced
½ tsp salt

Heat the oil in a large frying pan over a medium–high heat. Add the sliced shallots and sprinkle with the salt. Fry for about 10 minutes, stirring regularly until the shallots are crispy brown. Transfer to a paper towel to soak up any excess oil and use as a garnish. These are best used crispy right out of the oil.

# FRIED GARLIC
MAKES 60G (8 TBSP)

**This garnish might be simple but it's a great way of adding a nice garlicky flavour whenever you want a hit of garlic – it's often used to garnish noodle dishes. As you will see from the recipe, it's nothing fancy. Feel free to scale this recipe up or down as required. The garlic is roughly chopped so that you get a nice golden brown colour on the exterior while turning the inside of the garlic soft.**

PREP TIME: 2 MINS
COOKING TIME: 5 MINS

500ml (2 cups) rapeseed (canola) oil
150g (1 cup) garlic cloves, roughly chopped
A pinch of salt (optional)

Heat the oil in a frying pan over a medium–high heat. When hot, stir in the garlic and let it simmer in the oil for about 5 minutes until it is just beginning to turn light brown. Be sure to stir it from time to time so that the garlic fries evenly. Be very careful not to burn the garlic; it just needs to be soft and golden brown. Once it turns light brown, it doesn't take long at all to burn so you will have to work fast.

Transfer with a slotted spoon to a paper towel to soak up any excess oil. Ensure all the oil is soaked up or your crispy garlic will become soggy. I like to add a pinch of salt for flavour but that is optional.

This fried garlic is best used right away but you can store it in an air-tight container for a couple of days to use as a garnish.

TIP
Don't throw that oil away. It is delicious garlic-infused oil that you can use in your cooking. It will keep at room temperature but is best used within a couple of weeks.

# DESSERTS AND DRINKS

I've been making Thai-style coconut ice cream
since I was a kid. It's one of those desserts I have
to order when I go out too.

Thailand is famous for its delicious desserts and
drinks, and rightly so! I was pleasantly surprised by
the immense selection on offer when I first visited the
country. Here I have just touched on the fantastic desserts
and drinks found in Thailand. The following are some
of the most popular options featured on the menus
at Western Thai restaurants.

# SWEET STICKY RICE WITH MANGO
SERVES 4

There are some amazing desserts that come from Thailand. Many are quite complicated and call for ingredients that aren't easy to come by. That might be why the desserts offered at most Western Thai restaurants are rather limited. Sweet sticky rice and mango is one dessert recipe you are almost sure to find when you go out for a Thai meal. It's easy to make and can be made ahead of time, which is a bonus. In my opinion, some Thai desserts are very sweet but then I don't really have a sweet tooth. The salted coconut sauce balances the dessert nicely but add the sugar slowly and taste as you go, adding more or less to taste. I like to top this with toasted moong beans for texture. Any fresh mangoes will do for this recipe but I like to use the small yellow-skinned mangoes found at many Asian grocers.

PREP TIME: 20 MINS,
PLUS SOAKING TIME
COOKING TIME: 40 MINS

225g (1 generous cup) glutinous
   rice (this is gluten-free – see
   note on page 141)
250ml (1 cup) coconut milk
1 tsp salt
7 tbsp sugar (more or less
   to taste)
3 mangoes, thinly sliced
   and chilled

FOR THE SALTED
COCONUT SAUCE
150ml (⅔ cup) coconut milk
1 tbsp rice flour
½ tsp salt
1 tbsp sugar

OPTIONAL GARNISH
3 tbsp washed slit moong beans
½ tsp rapeseed (canola) oil

Pour the glutinous rice into a large bowl and cover with water. Swirl it around with your hand – the water will turn milky white. Strain and repeat a few times until the water runs almost clear. Cover with water again and allow to soak for 6 hours or overnight. Place the soaked rice in a steamer and steam for 20–25 minutes.

If using the toasted moong beans as a garnish, you might as well get this done while your sticky rice is steaming. Rinse the moong beans in water and then simmer in a saucepan of water for 10 minutes, then drain. Heat a frying pan that has been lightly greased with the oil over a medium heat. Add the moong beans and toast them for a couple of minutes until lightly browned. Be sure to move them around in the pan so that they toast evenly. Set aside.

Meanwhile, put the 250ml (1 cup) of coconut milk, salt and sugar in a saucepan and bring to a simmer. Cook for a few minutes until the sugar and salt have dissolved. Taste and adjust by adding more salt or sugar to taste. Keep warm. When the rice is cooked, stir it into this coconut milk mixture and let sit, covered, for 45 minutes.

To make the salted coconut sauce, whisk 2 tablespoons of the coconut milk with the rice flour into a smooth paste and set aside. Put the remaining sauce ingredients into a saucepan and bring to a simmer. Stir in the paste and continue simmering for a couple of minutes until smooth and thickened.

To serve, divide the sticky rice between four serving plates. Divide the sliced mango equally on the side of the rice and drizzle with the salted coconut sauce. Garnish with the toasted moong beans if using.

# 'STIR-FRIED' ROLLED ICE CREAM
SERVES 1–2

This is a way of making and presenting ice cream that is all Thai! It isn't actually stir-fried but frozen in a way that resembles stir-frying at Thai street-food stalls. The ice-cream mixture is frozen on ice-cold large metal discs with ingredients such as chocolate and other sweets that are chopped into the mixture with two sharp cutters. Then it's all spread out thinly so that it freezes. Lastly it is scraped off into ice-cream rolls. Although nowhere near the show, you can make these ice-cream rolls at home. In this recipe I made chocolate-chip ice cream but you could chop up and add your ingredients of choice. You will need a baking tray and a sharp metal spatula for this recipe.

PREP TIME: 5 MINS
FREEZING TIME: 2 HOURS

250ml (1 cup) double (heavy) cream
125ml (½ cup) condensed milk
1 tsp vanilla extract
2 generous handfuls of milk or dark chocolate chips (more or less to taste)

Pour the double (heavy) cream, condensed milk and vanilla extract into a mixing bowl and whisk to combine the ingredients. If your chocolate chips are large, finely chop them. Stir this into the mixture.

Pour the mixture onto a baking tray. Mine is 40 x 23cm (16 x 9in) so something similar in size will do. It is important not to fill it too deep. I usually aim for a layer of the creamy mixture that is no more than 3mm (⅛ inch) deep so that the frozen ice cream rolls better and more easily.

Place your filled baking tray in the freezer, being careful to keep it level, and freeze for about 2 hours.

Once the ice cream has frozen, take the tray out of the freezer. Slice the ice cream with a knife in segments that are the same width as the metal spatula you are using to roll the ice cream.

Use the sharp metal spatula to slowly scrape the ice cream off the tray. As you do this, the ice cream will roll up. Your rolls will be the same width as the spatula you use.

Serve immediately in dessert bowls for best results, or you can place the rolled ice cream in a container with a tight-fitting lid to store in the freezer.

# DAIRY-FREE THAI COCONUT ICE CREAM
SERVES 6

Thais don't eat a lot of dairy and this non-dairy coconut ice cream is very popular. The problem with making ice creams this way is that they freeze really hard. If you have an ice-cream maker, this recipe is easy. I recommend planning ahead so that you can serve the ice cream straight from the ice-cream maker rather than having to put it in the freezer. If you do freeze it, take it out about an hour before serving so that it has time to defrost. You can also make this ice cream by placing it in a bowl in the freezer and whisking it every half an hour or so until you are happy with it.

Be sure to taste the ice-cream mixture before placing it in your ice-cream maker or freezer. You can adjust the sweetness to taste.

PREP TIME: 10 MINS
FREEZING TIME: 4 HOURS
(LESS IN AN ICE-CREAM
MAKER)

750ml (3 cups) thick coconut milk (shake before opening)
3 tbsp grated palm sugar
5 tbsp white caster sugar
3 tbsp cornflour (cornstarch)
1 tsp vanilla extract, or the beans from 1 vanilla pod
Toasted coconut flakes, to serve (optional)

Pour 70ml (¼ cup) of the coconut milk into a bowl and set aside. Pour the rest into a saucepan and stir in the sugars. Bring to a simmer, stirring continuously until the sugars dissolve. Meanwhile, whisk the cornflour (cornstarch) into the coconut milk in the bowl until smooth.

When the sugar in the pan has dissolved, add the vanilla and stir it together. Taste it and add more sugar if needed. Add the coconut milk/cornflour mixture and continue simmering for a couple of minutes until the liquid is thick enough to coat the back of a wooden spoon.

If you don't have an ice-cream machine, place the liquid in a rectangular container that is large enough to hold it all. Place in the freezer and let it freeze for 2 hours. Stir well, then freeze for another 2 hours, stirring every 30 minutes until you have a soft and delicious ice cream.

If using an ice-cream maker, pour the liquid into the container, following the manufacturer's instructions. You may need to make it in a couple of batches if your ice cream maker isn't big enough to contain it all. Churn until it is soft but looks like ice cream. Serve immediately, scattered with toasted coconut flakes if you like.

This ice cream can be stored in the freezer for a good month. Just remember that it gets rock hard when frozen, so you will need to remove it from the freezer about an hour before serving.

# THAI ICED TEA
## SERVES 2 – 4

# THAI ICED COFFEE
## SERVES 4

The famous orange-coloured Thai iced tea so popular at Thai restaurants is soon to be (if not already) history. This is because the Thai black tea leaves used to make it were actually dyed with orange food colouring, which has now been banned. Not to worry, though; there isn't any flavour in that dye anyway. This recipe may not get you the beautiful orange colour but it will still taste the same. If you really want the orange glow, you could always add a little orange food colouring yourself. The non-orange version of this drink is pictured on page 4.

PREP TIME: 30 MINS
COOKING TIME: 10 MINS

5 tbsp sugar (more or less to taste)
5 Thai black tea bags
½ tsp vanilla extract
2 star anise
2 green cardamom pods, smashed
3 cloves
Ice cubes
250ml (1 cup) sweetened condensed milk

Pour 1 litre (4 cups) of water and the sugar into a saucepan and bring to a boil. Add the tea bags, vanilla and spices and simmer over a medium heat for 3 minutes. Turn off the heat and allow to cool for about 30 minutes. This can all be done ahead of time.

Remove the tea bags and strain out the spices, then chill the tea in the fridge until ready to serve.

Fill each glass with ice and pour the cold tea over the ice, leaving room at the top for the condensed milk. You'll just need to do this by eye but, generally speaking, I use 3 tablespoons of condensed milk per glass if serving four, and double that if serving two.

You can either serve the tea with the condensed milk floating on the top, or stir well to combine into a creamy mixture. If you want the condensed milk to float, place a spoon over the cold tea and slowly pour in the condensed milk.

This is a delicious and eye-catching way to serve Thai coffee. Now, as coffee is one of those drinks that people get really picky about, I'm not going to tell you how to brew coffee. You could use a bean-to-cup machine like I do, a cafetière or whatever floats your boat. Find the coffee beans you prefer and prepare the coffee as you normally do and all should be fine.

PREP TIME: 20 MINS

2 cardamom pods, smashed
5 tbsp sugar (more or less to taste)
1 tsp vanilla or almond extract (or a mixture of both)
1 litre (4 cups) freshly brewed hot coffee
Crushed ice
250ml (1 cup) sweetened condensed milk

Place the cardamom pods, sugar and vanilla/almond extract into the hot coffee and stir until the sugar has dissolved. Allow to cool and then fish out and discard the cardamom pods. Place the coffee in the fridge until ready to serve.

To serve, fill four 250ml (8fl oz) glasses with the crushed ice. Divide the coffee mixture between the four glasses, leaving room at the top for the condensed milk. If you want the condensed milk to float on top, place a spoon just above the coffee in the glass and slowly pour the condensed milk in. You could also just stir it all up.

# INDEX

# ACKNOWLEDGEMENTS

It has been a pleasure to work with everyone at Quadrille again to produce this cookbook. Thank you to Sarah Lavelle for commissioning the book and to copy editor Clare Sayer and my editor Louise Francis for all of their help with my words.

As always, it was great to work with photographer Kris Kirkham again. He has an amazing talent for getting the recipe photos just right! I would also like to thank food stylist Rosie Reynolds for making the recipes look so good on the plate! I have been working with both Kris and Rosie since my first cookbook and feel we are a real team now. Thank you!

We are so lucky to have so many top-notch Thai restaurants and takeaways in the UK, US and the rest of the Western world. I was inspired at a young age to replicate the dishes I tried at Thai restaurants, and my passion for the cuisine is stronger than ever. I learned a great deal from so many restaurants, and this book is my way of honouring them. I feel I have so much more to learn and can't wait to revisit my favourite Thai restaurants and discover new restaurants for inspiration and, of course, delicious meals.

Thank you to my literary agent, Clare Hulton. This is my sixth book and she made it all happen.

I would also like to thank my wife, Caroline, for putting up with my food obsession! She now works with me to test recipes, cooking when I'm writing and giving me her feedback. This book was made better by her and all the hard work she has done ensuring my written recipes actually work for those who read and then cook them.

This year I started a new Facebook group – Curry Chit Chaat. Through this group I have been in touch with members who try out my recipes and offer excellent feedback. Many of the recipes in this book were tested first on my blog and in the group. Thank you so much to everyone who helped me with their honest and helpful advice. You helped make this book happen!

Lastly, I would like to thank you for picking up this cookbook. I hope you enjoy reading and cooking from it as much as I have enjoyed developing the recipes and writing the book.

Publishing Director: Sarah Lavelle
Project Editor: Louise Francis
Junior Designer: Alicia House
Cover Design: Smith & Gilmour
Photographer: Kris Kirkham
Photography Assistant: Eyder Rosso Gonçalves
Food Stylist: Rosie Reynolds
Food Stylist Assistants: Sonali Shah and Troy Willis
Props Stylist: Faye Wears
Head of Production: Stephen Lang
Production Controller: Nikolaus Ginelli

First published in 2021 by Quadrille,
an imprint of Hardie Grant Publishing

Quadrille
52–54 Southwark Street,
London SE1 1UN
quadrille.com

Text © 2021 Dan Toombs
Photography © 2021 Kris Kirkham
Design and layout © 2021 Quadrille

Cataloguing-in-Publication Data. A catalogue record for this book is available from the British Library.

ISBN 978-1-78713-614-4

Reprinted in 2021 (twice)
10 9 8 7 6 5 4 3

Printed in China

FSC
www.fsc.org
MIX
Paper from responsible sources
FSC™ C020056

In five short years Dan took The Curry Guy from an idea to a reliable brand. The recipes are all developed and tested in Dan's home kitchen. And they work. His bestselling first cookbook – *The Curry Guy* – and the 250,000 curry fans who visit his blog every month can testify to that fact.

Dan holds regular cooking classes in North Yorkshire. Dates and times can be found on his website: www.greatcurryrecipes.net

If you have any recipe questions you can contact Dan (@thecurryguy) on Twitter, Facebook or Instagram.